CW00430896

Hans Rall · Michael Petzet · Franz Merta
King Ludwig II
Reality and Mystery

Hans Rall · Michael Petzet

King Ludwig II

Reality and Mystery

With an overview of the King's sojourns in residences,
castles and mountain lodges
by *Franz Merta*

SCHNELL + STEINER

Photo credits:

The pictures with inventory numbers are, if not stated otherwise, in possession of the King Ludwig II Museum at Herrenchiemsee. It is part of the Bayerische Schlösserverwaltung (BSV) and has partly exhibits on loan from the Wittelsbacher Ausgleichfonds (WAF).

Front cover: see picture on p 73
Back cover: see picture on p 74

Die Deutsche Bibliothek - Cataloguing in Publication Data:
King Ludwig II : reality and mystery / Hans Rall ; Michael Petzet. With an overview of the King's sojourns in residences, castles and mountain lodges / by Franz Merta. [Gesamtw. engl. transl. by Leslie Owen ...]. - Regensburg : Schnell und Steiner, 2001
Einheitssacht.: König Ludwig II. <engl.>
ISBN 3-7954-1427-X

The biography of King Ludwig II was compiled by Prof. Hans Rall, former Chief Archivist of the Privy Household Archives (Geheimes Hausarchiv). Prof. Michael Petzet selected the illustrations from pictorial documentation in the possession of the Bayerische Verwaltung der Staatlichen Schlösser, Gärten und Seen, some of which has never been published before, and also wrote the essay on the Kingís relationship with the arts. Dr. Franz Merta compiled the overview of the sojourns and its introduction.

English translation by Leslie Owen (essay Rall), Anthony Rich (appendix Rall) and Veronica Leary (essays Petzet and Merta).

© 2001 by Verlag Schnell & Steiner, Regensburg
All rights reserved
Typography, plates: Visuelle Medientechnik, Regensburg
Printed and bound by Erhardi Druck GmbH, Regensburg
Printed in Germany
ISBN 3-7954-1427-X

Contents

"You seem to think that I am unhappy. That's not so. For the most part I am happy and satisfied, namely when I am in the country or in the wonderful mountains. I am only miserable and distressed, often very melancholic, in the unhappy city. I can not live in the atmosphere of a tomb, I need to breathe the air of freedom. Just as the alpine rose pales and droops in marsh air, so I am incapable of living without the light of the sun and the soothing breezes of fresh air! To live here long (in the city) would be the death of me."

Ludwig II to Mrs Marie von Dahn-Hausmann
April 25th, 1876, 2:00 a.m.

Hans Rall

The Life and Death of King Ludwig II

The threads of fate

In the long dynasty of the Wittelsbachs, who assumed the throne of Bavaria in 1180 and of the Palatinate in 1214, we encounter a number of very similar personalities, but also figures unique in character.[1] Among the tombs in the crypt of St. Michael's in Munich, three remind the visitor of highly notable rulers: Duke William V was the most pious; his son, Elector Maximilian I, was politically the most important; King Ludwig II,[2] however, is to this day the most popular.

The handsome, if somewhat enigmatic King, who acceded to the throne in March 1864 when not quite 19 years of age, showed no sign of the unfortunate genealogical antecedents – today obvious genetic consequences of consanguinity[3] – which caused a disastrous concentration of schizophrenic tendencies derived in a recessive hereditary process from several ruling Houses. We have proof that these tendencies are traceable in the paternal and maternal lines to Duke William of Brunswick-Wolfenbüttel (d. 1592), although neither the King's great-great-grandfather Prince Frederick Michael of Zweibrücken, a successful Imperial Field-Marshal, nor his descendants were adversely affected by them. Neither the political acumen of the first King of Bavaria, Max I, nor the energetic rule of the gifted Ludwig I, nor the scholarly leanings of Max II, Ludwig II's father, betrayed schizophrenic characteristics. Ludwig's mother, Princess Marie of Prussia, whose portrait her father-in-law had had painted for his Gallery of Beauties, was an unassuming woman of a kindliness verging on self-effacement. Happy as Max and Marie were in their married life, it was their very union that was to prove disastrous for their two children, for pathological symptoms also appeared in their younger son Otto, being evident by 1875, but in different and more serious form. Occasional remarks subsequently made by Ludwig regarding his late father and widowed mother evince such sombre aversion that the scientifically interested monarch may well be supposed to have suspected the unwelcome genetic implications of his parents' union.

The alienists' report of June 8th, 1886, draws attention to the "established" fact that Princess Alexandra, an aunt of King Ludwig II, had been "for many years" – until her death in 1875 – "the victim of an incurable mental complaint". The reality was in this case by no means so unproblematical. Alexandra, whose portrait had been painted for the gallery of her father, Ludwig I, who made beauty and virtue the conditions of inclusion, was a poetess who also adapted children's stories for the stage and became a popular authoress. She devoted herself to youth and was an early contributor to Isabella Braun's youth periodicals.[4] In her "Phantasie- und Lebensbildern" she presented excellent free translations from French and English. Often, however, she imagined that her head was weighed down by a heavy object – a piano. A similar trouble afflicted Ludwig II, who used to relieve headaches with an ice-bag. His maternal grandfather, Prince William of Prussia (1783–1851), who is not mentioned in the medical expertise, was admittedly an unusually circumspect commander under York in the Wars of Liberation – he persuaded the latter to fall in with the King's policy – and also a contented husband and father. However, he displayed a growing tendency towards seclusion and indecision, especially after losing his adored wife and his promising son Waldemar. His look resembles that of his Bavarian grandson. Ludwig's great-great-uncle Charles Augustus, Duke of Zweibrücken from 1775 to 1795, was not only a man of great artistic taste, but also embarked on architectural projects far in excess of his financial resources. Though very astute, he possessed highly unorthodox traits of character. Ludwig's parents were unaware of the problematic genetic legacy from both sides, but approached the upbringing of their two sons with great care and affection. They could not avert the latter's subsequent schizophrenic tendencies – a problem detected at an early stage by their family physician, Dr. von Gietl. Hereditary diseases are more common than is generally known.

From the educational point of view, it was not without significance that the parents were familiar with the paternal admonitions of the first Elector to his son and successor – Max by virtue of a book dedication by his Divinity tutor Oettl at his First Communion in 1827, Marie from a reference by the Keeper of the King's Archives, Professor Soeltl. The child himself displayed inclinations of his own.

While still a child, Ludwig would build imaginatively with bricks; his development went beyond the hour-for-hour schedule of daily activities laid down – with occasional handwritten emendations – by his father. In this system, too, the interest of the parents in their children was evidenced by the fact that they were together with their mother during the late morning and at lunch. Ludwig's curriculum included at all ages Religious Instruction, as from June 1863 Logic, and as from July the History of Philosophy by a tutor only ten years older – Johannes Huber who used to meet the young King twice a week in the winter of 1864–1865 for discussions on philosophical and general problems raised by his young pupil. The German language was cultivated in the form of literary history and reading. It was possibly this initiation that made the King an unusually keen and versatile reader in later years. Bavarian History was an independent subject. Ludwig developed a notable proficiency in the classical and modern languages – especially French, thanks to the encouragement of his tutor Franz Trautmann, the father of Karl Trautmann, the famous Munich cultural history specialist. Many years later he was still able to recite by heart – and with due expression – long passages from German and French classics. Nor were Mathematics, Physical and Political Geography and Astronomy neglected. There is evidence that Ludwig had piano lessons three times a week at least from October 1858 until autumn 1860 – with a teacher whom Ludwig admittedly rejected and who later delivered a biased verdict by way of revenge. Even at that time Ludwig showed a general interest in opera; he attended Wagner's Lohengrin in 1861 with his parents and grandfather. The comprehensive weekly time-table also required Ludwig to draw, swim and ride; dancing and fencing were added as from 1859. This was the time at which Ludwig was commissioned lieutenant; in the winter of 1859–1860 he had regular weapons training, as from 1862 lessons in military science, and in the winter of 1861–1862 also an hour of drill such as he had already experienced in 1855 at the age of ten or eleven. At his majority he became a colonel and was sworn in by his father on the Constitution. He had not been attending university lectures by Liebig, Jolly, Johannes Huber and others for long when he lost his father.

Early events: 1864–65

First political decisions

First Max II had died in the middle of a positively desperate conflict with Archduke Albert, the representative of the Emperor Francis Joseph, over the independence of the Elbe duchies (Schleswig-Holstein),[5] which were being treated as a political pawn by the victorious powers Austria and Prussia. The dying King had upheld his final decision to the last, so that Germany's two great powers did not succeed at the German Bundestag in Frankfurt in referring the Elbe duchies issue to a committee. The legacy of the deceased ruler was regarded as sacrosanct. Together with Württemberg and Hesse, Bavaria was at that time struggling to prevent a collapse of the German Zollverein – in which the Bavarian Foreign Minister, von Schrenck, had admittedly ceased to have much confidence. Austria itself had by its inconsistency caused untold harm to the economic front in central Europe, and had unintentionally played into the hands of Prussian policy. Between the young King and his Foreign Minister a difference of opinion arose over the customs union issue. When von Schrenck tendered his resignation it was accepted all the more readily because he had not consented to Cabinet Secretary von Pfistermeister becoming a State Counsellor. On December 4th, 1864, Ludwig II appointed Baron von der Pfordten[6] Foreign Minister, although the latter had been dropped by Max II in 1859 to appease the Second Chamber. In doing so the young King was actuated not by any special liKing, but by a sound appraisal of the political record of his father's Minister, who had for years furthered a policy of compromise between Austria, the power holding the presidency of the German Confederation, and Prussia, and had thus strengthened Bavaria's position within Germany. Whereas after the Prussian victory over Austria in 1866[7] the German Confederation dissolved itself and Bavaria was obliged to conclude a defensive and offensive alliance with Prussia – its decisions of foreign policy thus being largely dictated – it was still able up to that date to take comparatively free decisions. At that time its young King was chiefly interested in the despatches from his envoys – for the possibilities of Bavarian foreign policy. Von der Pfordten himself had misgivings about reassuming the foreign portfolio, as he was apprehensive of the majority in the Second Chamber, but also of that in the First Chamber, whose blueblooded members regarded him as an intruder. Bavaria's democrats – admittedly not numerous – and the recently founded Bavarian Progressive Party lodged objections to Pfordten's appointment, while the conservative press and the "Bayerischer Volksbote" supported him. He was also favoured by the Austrian government. Pfordten, who had already been approached by representatives of the late King early in 1864 to resume charge of the ministry, accepted the young ruler's assignment.

In 1864 Ludwig II took a number of clear, independent and prompt decisions of far-reaching significance. He had already – upon Schrenck's final resignation – chosen not to continue the combination of the Ministry of Commerce and Public Works with the Foreign and Crown Affairs portfolios as had been the case since 1849. Instead, he entrusted it on January 1st, 1865 to Adolph von Pfretzschner, who was later to make a mark as Finance Minister, and as from August 1st, 1866 – and thus an unusually difficult time – to Gustav von Schlör[8] from the Upper Palatinate, a devotee of social, economic and technical progress and Austro-German union. As early as July 29th, 1864 he dismissed his circumspect Minister of Education, von Zwehl, who had been conducting a personal correspondence with Catholic bishops, and replaced him with Nikolaus von Koch, for many years a senior ministerial official and hitherto Provincial President of Upper Franconia, who was more reserved with regard to ecclesiastical aspirations. Almost simultaneously, on August 1st, he appointed a new Minister of Justice: Eduard von Bomhard, a Deputy and former Chief Public Prosecutor who was also jointly engaged on a German code of civil procedure. On assuming office he was required to declare the retention of the Royal chancellery compatible with continental constitutionalism.

This was the King who despatched his Cabinet Secretary in May 1864 to secure the services of Richard Wagner[9] – for whom this meant salvation. As Crown Prince he had attended a Munich performance of "Lohengrin" with his father and grand-father, and had ever since wished to encourage Wagner's musical drama: "The earnestness of art must suffuse all things." He wished above all to cure Munich theatre-goers of their predilection for the frivolous and the tendentious; Shakespeare, Calderón, Mozart, Gluck and Weber were to raise them to a sublime and contemplative state of mind in preparation for the experience of Wagnerian opera. Thanks to the King's generous financial support and to his enthusiastic sympathy and friendship, Wagner's first performance of "Tristan und Isolde" on June 10th, 1865 proved to be a climax in the unity of music and poetry. In his encouragement of Richard Wagner's drama, but also of the stage in general, Ludwig displayed the energy of a veritable theatre director. In 1864 he had made Karl von Perfall Court Music Director, and in 1867 entrusted him with the Directorship of the Court Theatre. The building opened in 1865 and is known today as the Gärtnerplatz-Theater, the foundation stone of which was laid in the first year of Ludwig's reign, was intended in his own words to be for the capital "a popular theatre in the true sense of the term", to counteract "the corrupting influence of fifth-rate theatricals" and to promote "popular culture". He often went there himself. A Schiller enthusiast while still Crown Prince, he insisted as King, particularly in the case of "Maria Stuart" or "Wilhelm Tell", on an appropriate stage interpretation. Performances of French classics, too – Molière or Corneille – reached a new peak of excellence under his aegis. In 1882 he caused Perfall to stage Shakespeare's "Pericles, Prince of Tyre", a play performed for the last time in England 250 years before – and in Germany not at all. As from the late 1860's Ludwig II preferred plays about the Bourbons and their times, but also encouraged Spanish classics and themes. In addition to German and English themes, there were also occasional stagings on Russian and Indian subjects. Ludwig II made a concession to contemporary social criticism when he caused Ibsen's "Pretenders" to be performed in 1875 and the same author's "Vikings of Helgeland" on April 10th, 1876

– both in his Court Theatre. This was thus the first German stage to produce a work of Ibsen, and Ludwig II anticipated Duke George II of Saxe-Meiningen in initiating the discussion on this author in the German theatrical world. According to Erika Wilk, not a few of his theatre promotions were part of a dialogue with himself.[10]

At the private performances held in the Royal Bavarian Court and National Theatre as from 1864 during the normal evening hours, Ludwig ordered the staging not only of Wagner's works, but also of other operas of repute, such as those by Auber, Gluck, Goldmark, Massenet, Meyerbeer, Mozart, Reinthaler, Verdi and Weber. The King likewise desired these command performances to be supplemented by the theatrical music of Grandaur, Mendelssohn, Perfall and Schumann. It is interesting to note the independence of the King's judgement when in 1865 – the year of Wagner's great triumph – the composer Max Zenger (1837–1911) voiced apprehensions about the effect of Wagner's music on the art. He argued that it was likely to be prejudicial to music as an independent art if Wagner's innovative principles were to be extended to all fields of music as a result of false assessment by his successors. To this the young King replied: "That is one point of view. Mine is different, but I am most grateful to you for showing such candour to your King. Let it always be so!" In 1879 Ludwig gave him a teaching assignment at the Munich Royal School of Music. From 1880 to 1882 he commissioned him, as an outstanding expert on period music, to write the score for three historical ballets set in the reigns of Louis XIV and XV of France. Ludwig II's appreciation of Zenger's achievements, of which he had precise knowledge from the private performances, was so great that in 1882 he appointed him Regius Professor of Music.

At the same time the King was anxious to entrust Gottfried Semper, the most distinguished architect of the time and already noted for his Court Theatre in Dresden and for the reconstruction of Vienna, with the development of Munich into an impressive modern capital. Two major thoroughfares were to run from west to east one from the Central Station to the Court and National Theatre, the other from the north-east corner of the Residenz across the Isar to a Wagner Festival Theatre. An alliance of the cabinet, the municipality and the citizens succeeded in thwarting the King's plans. This lack of sympathy embittered the King all the more in view of the current – and growing – anti-Wagner trend in Munich: legitimate criticism, but also calumniation of the "drain" on Royal cabinet funds, of the Dresden "revolutionary". If the youthful King did write over-expansive letters to the composer, he was still concern primarily with the realization of his oeuvre.[11] On August 27th, 1865 Wagner completed his draft of "Parsifal". For the King, this work is "sacred", is in the "purest and noblest sense religious". Ludwig identifies the temple of the Holy Grail with the monastery church at Ettal – a favourite resort of his.

On November 11th, 1865 Wagner arrived at Hohenschwangau on a visit to the King. On the following Sunday morning Wagner caused ten oboists from an infantry regiment to serenade his Royal host with a passage from "Lohengrin" from various towers of the castle. Every evening twenty regimental music conducted by the guest would play the latter's works, but also those of Gluck, Weber and Beethoven. In the castle Wagner himself also played to the King. The activities of Wagner's enemies went on, however. The clergy denounced him heathen. The ruler's grandfather, ex-King Ludwig I (who was on reasonably good terms with his grandson), the Queen Mother and his Minister von der Pfordten were all worried lest the King should neglect his state duties. When the opposition to Wagner reached the point at which the police no longer felt able to guarantee his safety, the King could not but request him to leave Munich for a few months, which he did on December 10th, 1865.[12] By then Wagner and his activities had cost Ludwig's cabinet fund 190,000 gulden. His salary from this source was 8,000 gulden, that of a Minister (from the public purse) 4,000 gulden.

The year 1866

The King was embittered over Wagner's enforced departure and vented his displeasure on the warners in his entourage. On von der Pfordten, in particular, he was nevertheless dependent. After the conclusion of the Gastein convention between Austria and Prussia on August 20th, 1865, by which notwithstanding the administrative partition of the Elbe duchies Bismarck achieved the aim of their annexation by Prussia, King Ludwig II requested his Foreign Minister to prepare a memorandum. It gave him to understand that Bavaria, being unable to count on Austria, was now called upon to seek an understanding with Prussia. Neither von der Pfordten nor the Minister of War nor the King's Adjutant-General believed in an Austrian victory over Prussia. The King was so appalled that Pfordten actually witnessed him taking a keen interest in state affairs. The possibility of a war between Prussia and Austria, "these twin pillars of Germany", horrified him. He found it unthinkable that his close relationship with one of the two ruling Houses might be ended, and therefore urged his Minister to settle the differences. Later, too, the King emphasized to Pfordten that he wanted peace, but the latter had to reply that this was no longer a matter of desires. Austria, whose clumsy and expensive war machine was slow in getting into its stride, commenced secret preparations for mobilization on February 28th, 1866. Prussia started a partial mobilization on March 28th. When Austria itself repudiated Bavaria's good offices in an approach to Prussia on April 6th, Ludwig had a meeting on April 11th with Prince Chlodwig von Hohenlohe-Schillingsfürst, an exponent of a German settlement excluding Austria. The King was apprehensive about the Prussian desire for a German parliament, as he feared for Bavaria's independence. The Prussian proposal had been turned down by his Foreign Minister on April 9th. When Hohenlohe assured the King that Prussia was now seeking supremacy only in northern Germany, he interrupted him: "Now, but later they will be wanting even more." It is nevertheless significant that the King was already prepared to consult the man who advocated co-operation with Prussia and recommended neutrality instead of war. After the lost war the King sent for him again. It is not surprising that the King did not now play a more prominent role. At first he was inclined to abdi-

Linderhof, the King's favourite palace,
illustration by Heinrich Berling

cate rather than sign the mobilization order proposed by the Cabinet the day before; at the Bamberg conference of Kingdoms and major Grand Duchies his Foreign Minister was still working for peace on May 14th. Bavaria's position between Austria and Prussia was desperate. Referring, among other matters, to the opening of the Landtag, the ceremonious nature of which he found distasteful, the King mentioned to his legal adviser Lutz that he wished to abdicate in favour of his brother Otto, as his mental health was not satisfactory. Although this may have been largely a pretext for evading responsibility for a war in which defeat was a foregone conclusion, the fact deserves to be recorded.

As the Bavarian army was no match for the Prussian in armament – a result of the attitude of the Second Chamber – its function was purely defensive. The Bavarian Chief of Staff therefore signed an agreement with Austria at Olmütz on June 8th, under which Bavaria was to render assistance only if Austria was attacked. As against Bismarck's draft constitutions of June 10th, however, von der Pfordten clung to the Austrian connection. On June 16th he vainly sought the support of the German Confederation for an appeal to the two German Great Powers to evacuate Holstein. As early as June 14th Prussia had accused the majority of the Confederation of violating its Articles by being a party to a declaration of war on a member State. On June 16th the German Confederation decided – as the attacked party and not as the aggressor – on war. There followed on July 2nd a appeal by King Ludwig II to the Bavarian population for the "preservation of the whole of Germany as a free and powerful unit, and for the maintenance of Bavaria as an independent and worthy component of the great German Fatherland". The appeal took into account the widespread readiness – present also in the Royal family – not to abandon Austria in its struggle against Prussia. Ludwig's great-uncle, Prince Charles, was Commander-in-Chief. The King, who had not opened the Landtag until after his birthday visit to Wagner in Switzerland, had been present in Munich not at the despatch of the troops, but nevertheless at the departure of the Generals, and on June 25th visited the headquarters and the troops in Bamberg. In the meantime, aloof from current events, he spent his time at Schloss Berg and on the Roseninsel. On July 28th, after the war was lost, Bavaria, too, concluded an armistice with Prussia; it was to come

into force on August 2nd. Bavaria's situation was deplorable: no prelimi-
naries of peace had been agreed upon, Prussian troops continued to fight
in Bavaria and occupied Würzburg and Nuremberg. King Ludwig now
despatched a Bavarian diplomat, Baron Perglas, to Paris with a handwritten communication to Napoleon III – who, however, did not receive
him until August 15th In his reply of August 27th, Napoleon told the
defeated King that he had done his utmost to moderate the Prussian
demands, although this had not been easy in view of German national
susceptibilities. On the part of a ruler sympathetic to German unity the
request for French aid, so far from tending towards separatism, was an act
of sheer self-defence. Von der Pfordten was meanwhile negotiating with
Bismarck. When he telegraphed to Munich on August 19th to known
whether he and his delegation might conclude an alliance with Prussia on
the basis of guaranteed status and frontiers, even if this meant cession of
territory, Ludwig II placed the issue before the Council of Ministers. One
of their number, von Bomhard, informed the King at Schloss Berg of his
colleagues' affirmative decision. The King thereupon re-ventilated the
idea of seeking French intervention, and the Minister left no doubt that
this would mean the resignation of himself and his colleagues – apart from
the possible loss of the Palatinate as the price of such assistance. The King
therefore telegraphed to Pfordten and Bray-Steinburg on August 20th,
empowering them to come to terms with Prussia on the basis of
guaranteed status and frontiers. Even if called upon to cede territory, he
was more anxious to safeguard Bavaria's sovereignty than avert such losses. The Bavarian plenipotentiaries, however, did sign a treaty at midnight
on August 22nd – just before the expiration of the armistice – which
contained no explicit guarantee of Bavarian sovereignty.
The outcome of the war, which imposed upon Bavaria an indemnity of
30 million gulden, entailed not only a minor cession of territory and the
embarrassing demand for the surrender of the Elector John William's
Düsseldorf art collection, but also the enforced alliance with Prussia.
While the financial exactions were much resented – the surrender of the
paintings, now incorporated as Royal property in the general collection,
being on the other hand successfully postponed – the defeated young King
suffered under the loss of sovereignty involved in the inescapable defensive

and offensive alliance with the victors (subordination of the Bavarian army to the King of Prussia in the event of war) and under the restricted freedom of action resulting quite generally from the new situation. For a moment he considered abdicating in favour of Otto. In the autumn of 1866 he sought a religious and psychological sanction for his – theoretically still sovereign – status as King of Bavaria by the inclusion in the prescribed form of the Mass a daily prayer for the ruler throughout his kingdom – analogous to that said in Austria for the Emperor by virtue of the traditions of the old Empire, but also, since, 1857, in France for Napoleon III. Thus, in the hour of defeat the young King of Bavaria sought liturgical parity with the Emperors in Paris and Vienna – with the support of no less a person than the famous church historian and theologian Ignaz von Döllinger.[13] The Curia, however, was not amenable to Ludwig's wishes. In the fateful month of July 1866, when Ludwig commenced a new volume of his diary,[14] he was no doubt already thinking of the manifestation of his Royal status in terms of a religious – and patently visible – symbolism. On the cover we see a fortified castle resembling that later erected at Neuschwanstein, while the end-papers depict a crown over a sceptre and an orb, each surmounted by crosses, the whole being crowned by a bowl inscribed in Church Slavonic and appropriate lettering with the words: "This vessel be my aid, O Lord ...". The allusion is to the Grail castle, to the Bread and the Wine as the aim of preparations for confession which the Wittelsbach King, like other Catholic rulers, used to take upon himself, sometimes with the aid of diary entries. For Ludwig II invariably took confession and communion very seriously, especially after succeeding to the throne.

The decisive years: 1866–1876

In 1866 the King's life and work readied a highly critical turning-point. The divine might and right of Kings, whose mission he wished to serve, and whose solemnity and binding force lent moral strength to his personality whenever he consulted his conscience and formed his intentions, had to be upheld after outward defeat – at least in the encounter with domestic opponents. The period from 1866 to 1876 proved to be the decisive decade in the development of the unhappy ruler. He wished the composition of his government always to be such as to conform with political reality by measures in keeping with the demands of the times, and on the other hand to safeguard the Crown and State of Bavaria from democratic, socialistic and nationalistic tendencies. He knew very well that the decisions he took with the aid of his cabinet were attacked, and therefore wished to retain the energetic lawyer Johann Lutz, whom his father had appointed to the cabinet on a non-established basis shortly his death. In 1867 Ludwig was not on this account inclined to, make him Minister of Justice in place of von Bomhard – himself a keen champion of kingly authority – although on September 18th he was compelled to take this course. Diplomatic instructions and reports would on occasion call for his personal intervention, and ministerial documents likewise. Like his father and grandfather, he used to write signed notes communicating his own decisions; these might concern issues of principle, the legislative process, even the Ministry of War. This is shown in the recently published enquiry by Detlev Vogel, covering the period down to 1875.[15] The King received an insight into critical problems of the age in general from Johannes Huber, a philosophy professor whom he had known as Crown Prince. Certain allusions in the latter's work "Der Proletarier" fringed on Lassalle's ideas. Huber took up the problems of socialism, but had a critical approach to Darwin, Strauss and Haeckel. Crown Prince Rudolph of Austria, an expert on zoology, and especially ornithology, and a ruthless critic of ecclesiastical and political traditions, appears to have spared Ludwig nothing in their private exchange of ideas. Bismarck's solution of the "German question" in terms of power politics constantly called for reactions, many of them painful, by the King of Bavaria. For him the decade from 1866 to 1876 was thus full of existential problems impinging upon him from outside. But it was this decade, too, that involved him more and more in the struggle against the fate that threatened to emerge from his schizophrenic tendencies. The last decade of his life was to bring the final disintegration of a man still young in years, strong of will, and of great actual talent.

After defeat: new possibilities and influences

In autumn 1866 the King, committed as he was to the alliance with Prussia, was confronted with the question of how far Bavaria could still cooperate with Austria and the other south German States. The outcome of the war seemed a refutation of von der Pfordten's policy. The King considered the merits of a number of men potentially capable of an effective political contribution including external relations. Ludwig was under the influence of various personalities: one, his grandfather Ludwig I, still thought highly of von der Pfordten and regarded his grandson's craze for Wagner as an aberration. On the other hand, a man closer to the King, his Master of the Horse Count Holnstein, reminded him of the mediatized Prince who on April 11th, 1866 had counselled neutrality rather than war. On December 31st, 1866 only a few weeks after Pfordten's dismissal, Hohenlohe was appointed by the King.[16] He at once discussed with him the possibilities for government on a tighter rein: he envisaged that instead of being President of the Council of Ministers – and thus of equal status with his colleagues, as had been the case since 1849 – he should be appointed Minister-President. This would enable Hohenlohe – as the King put it to keep them (the other Ministers) in order better". In 1867 a stormy session of the Council of Ministers did actually result in the Ministry of Justice changing hands in accordance with Hohenlohe's wishes: Lutz replaced Bomhard. This meant that the King was deprived of the strongest personality in the Cabinet Secretariat. Hohenlohe admittedly pursued the possibility of an independent southern Germany maintaining good relations with Prussia, but nevertheless indicated to the French

Envoy in Munich that in the event of possible military complications between Prussia and France the subjects of the King of Bavaria would insist on his implementing the defensive and offensive alliance with Prussia. Thus it was that in 1867 Württemberg successfully urged Bavaria to accept Bismarck's proposal for the reconstitution of the Zollverein – the resistance of the First Chamber to this measure being broken by Ludwig II. Incognito, like his grandfather, he visited the World Exhibition in Paris, where he made the acquaintance of the French Emperor. In August, when Napoleon III paid a visit to the Emperor Francis Joseph in Salzburg, Ludwig accompanied him for the part of his train journey between Augsburg and Rosenheim. On the way back Napoleon had a meeting with Hohenlohe. The Southern Confederation as envisaged by Napoleon and the new Austrian Chancellor Beust failed to materialize. However, patriotic circles in Bavaria – like their King – had the impression that the independence of the Crown and the sovereignty of the Kingdom were endangered. Bavarian patriots seemed to have been urging the King to favour a Southern Confederation. The King called upon Hohenlohe for a memorandum, and on November 23rd, 1867 he advised the formation of a union of south German States. This was actually desired by Hohenlohe as a means to an end, namely, for an organic connection with the North German Confederation. For months the grandfather had been counselling his grandson to re-appoint von der Pfordten, but Ludwig II replied evasively: Pfordten himself had said that the time was not ripe.

Betrothal; relationships with women

Long before Ludwig's betrothal, in a conversation with his Minister of Justice von Bomhard, a man with pronounced views on the principle of kingship, he referred to the ventilated urgency of marriage, and came to the conclusion. "I simply have no time to marry – that is Otto's business" (the latter's complaint did not become apparent until later). He nevertheless became betrothed to Sophie, daughter of Duke Max of ("in") Bavaria, who had been close to him since childhood and had shown him affection since

1862. He had once cast her as Gretchen in allotting the roles for a reading of "Faust". Later he was glad that she could play Wagner's works to him and shared his enthusiasm for the Master. His chivalrous attentions were construed by her parents as courtship. During a crisis in their relations brought about by Sophie's parents, he wrote to her in sombre allusion to a self-ordained fate: "My destiny is known to you; from Berg I once wrote to you about my mission. You know that I have not long to live, that I shall pass from this world when the unspeakable occurs, when my star ceases to shine, when the Beloved Friend is taken from me. Then indeed my time will end, and with it my right to live." Although Ludwig's sympathy for Wagner's fate was foremost in his words, an analogy with certain of his other utterances suggests that he identified the date of his death with the emergence of his affliction. We do not know since when he had been aware of the latter. Shortly after writing this letter he denied conjectures to the effect that his love for his betrothed was not sincere. In March 1867 he felt a "longing for marriage".[17] Plans for an Easter journey to Rome and Jerusalem were abandoned and supplanted by other travels, to some extent politically motivated, by political decisions and by meetings with Napoleon III – all such as to bring home to the loser of 1866 the truth about Bavaria's situation. In the course of this hectic year the relationship between Ludwig and Sophie cooled off. It may have come to his knowledge – of this there is no proof – that she had fallen in love with a Court photographer. In October 1867 he terminated the betrothal. He wrote to Sophie that pressure and interference on the part of her mother were distasteful; his heart was full of brotherly affection for her, but not of the love "necessary to the bond of marriage". Sophie's parents bore the ultimate responsibility for this broken engagement, seeing that they had been over-zealous in wishing to see childhood affection lead to marriage. The union would have been between a great-grandson and a granddaughter of the first King of Bavaria. Another possible marriage – not entertained by Ludwig despite the political advantages involved – was that sought by Queen Victoria of England in Spring 1870 for her daughter Louise.[18]

Ludwig II had close relationships with few women. Consanguinity and natural affinity united him with Sophie's elder sister, the Empress Elisabeth of Austria, who later feared that she too might fall a victim to the same complaint. Melancholic inclinations were common to King and Empress. The fact that Ludwig almost invariably experienced art manifestations and their executants as an integral unit brought him into close contact with Lila von Bulyowsky, who acted the title-role in "Maria Stuart", and with Josefine Scheffsky, a Court Theatre singer whose voice greatly pleased him. Feminine self-conceit, however, vitiated both relationships. With the actress Marie Dahn-Hausmann, on the other hand, the King maintained a heartfelt friendship that embraced even questions of religious scruple. When she told him that her daughter had suffered a mental disturbance while on her honeymoon, the King wrote on April 10th, 1878: "What I find incomprehensible is that this disaster should have overtaken your child precisely at a time of happiness and joy; rather is it moments of suffering and despair that bring about sickness of the mind." Partly political in motivation was the King's friendship with Tsarina Maria Alexandrovna, a Princess of Hesse-Darmstadt by birth and twenty-one years his senior. Ludwig had a meeting with the Russian Imperial couple, whose acquaintance he had made in 1864, at the Bavarian resort of Bad Kissingen in 1868 at the instance of his Minister Hohenlohe. The latter told the King that the friendship with the Imperial couple – "in view of the precarious situation of the German Kingdoms and major Grand Duchies, and especially of Bavaria, since the 1866 war" – was an "invaluable guarantee", as in the existing circumstances the Kingdom could not contract alliances with foreign Powers. Emotionally, too, the Tsarina had a stabilizing influence on Ludwig.

Symbols and manifestations of monarchy

Ludwig not only greatly respected the Russian Imperial couple, but was also captivated as early as 1866 by the mystery of the Orthodox liturgy, as we see from the beginning of a new diary dating from July of that year. Soon after his defeat in war the King set about the erection of his castles, which, like the splendid edifices of the 18th century, were not in the first instance the work of an architect, but that of a Royal patron. The King, with his sovereignty in danger since 1866, desired his architectural works to symbolize kingship. Thus Neuschwanstein, Linderhof and Herren-chiemsee came into being. The plans for buildings had long been elaborated and repeatedly revised before they were executed under his very precise supervision. His friendliness particularly to simple folk, as well as the great generosity towards the needy and the poor that is evidenced by the books of his Cabinet fund, show that one of his notions of kingship was that of a commitment to all men. He keenly supported the foundation of the Bavarian Red Cross by his mother, Queen Marie, in 1869. To her, too – as we know from numerous attentions – he remained close most of the time, and long after the great joint walking tour of the Tyrol in 1864.

Home and foreign policy 1869–1870

The important social reform laws introduced by the Hohenlohe Ministry were in part the completion of those already begun by Max II.[19] The army reform in imitation – and in the interest – of the Prussian ally caused resentment in Bavaria. When the new Minister of Education and Public Worship came out in favour of a liberal Education Bill (which had Ludwig's support) and against the impending proclamation of Papal Infallibility, this increased clerical mistrust of the Hohenlohe administration and led to an electoral victory of the Bavarian Patriotic Party in May 1869.[20] When the parties failed to reach agreement, the King dissolved the Second Chamber on October 6th, 1869 – to the delight of the Liberals. The General Election resulted in eighty seats for the Patriots, sixty-three for the Progressives, and eleven for independents who were virtually Liberals. Hohenlohe tendered his resignation, but the Munich Liberals urged the King not to dismiss the Ministry. On December 20th Ludwig II decided to keep Hohenlohe in office for the time being, and gave Lutz his second portfolio-education. The Patriots could not accept this government re-shuffle. Conscious of the danger of a new struggle, the King opened the

Landtag on January 17th, 1870 with a call for reconciliation. He spoke of faithful implementation of the alliance with Prussia, but also promised that he would countenance only such measures for the reorganization of Germany as entailed no danger for Bavaria's independence. The Humble Addresses of both Chambers, however, were clear expressions of no confidence in the Ministry. Ludwig accepted only that of the Second Chamber. This communication from the Deputies, drawn up by Dr. Jörg, states: "The people of Bavaria are constitutional by nature, but do not desire party government." The King reacted on March 8th, 1870 by replacing Hohenlohe – at his own recommendation – as Minister of Crown Affairs and Foreign Minister by Count Bray-Steinburg. With the backing of the British Envoy in Munich the latter proposed that the Great Powers mediate in the Franco-Prussian conflict arising out of the candidature of a south German, Catholic Hohenzollern prince for the Spanish throne.

The King and the war of 1870

When on July 14th the Prussian Minister enquired what Bavarian support Prussia could expect in the event of French aggression, the Bavarian Minister of War, von Pranckh, undertook without consulting the King to make Bavaria's two army corps available. On July 15th Bismarck notified Bavaria of the mobilization of the North German Confederation and requested that the armament of Bavaria be expedited. The very same day Pranckh despatched a Bavarian military plenipotentiary to Berlin. On this date, too, the Council of Ministers met and asked the King to order mobilization. On this crucial day it was evening before Ludwig II returned to Schloss Berg from a long mountain excursion; he had discussed the situation with his Cabinet Secretary before the Ministers' request reached him. He had desired a peaceful settlement of the conflict, and had by his absence supported Bray against Pranckh, but had also given consideration to the casus foederis – and no less to the consequences for Bavaria. When the Cabinet Secretary had left Schloß Berg in the small hours of the morning and the King had retired, the Ministers' emissary arrived, pointed

31

out how precious every hour was, and drew attention to the difficulties to be expected in the Chamber, particularly among the Ultramontanists, and to the restlessness in Munich. Ludwig II, who had received the emissary at his bedside, exclaimed: "My decision is taken. *Bis dat qui cito dat*".

Ludwig's political decisions after the victory at Sedan
Bavaria's financial and territorial claims

The King had taken a prompt and clearly calculated decision. After the decisive victory at Sedan his action was similar. On September 9th the Council of Ministers met. On the 12th they requested the somewhat reserved King for power to negotiate on a constitutional alliance. In the night of September 12th to the 13th the King received the visit of Bismarck's representative, Graf Tauffkirchen, a Bavarian who had just become Prefect of the Department of Meuse. Without delay – on the 13th – the King caused Count Bray-Steinburg to write to Bismarck expressing his readiness to send his representatives to the Prussian headquarters.[21] On the 17th, however, he instructed Bray-Steinburg to make discreet enquiries about the views and intentions prevailing in Dresden, Stuttgart, Karlsruhe and Darmstadt. On September 17th the King commissioned an exhaustive memorandum on the problem of a German constitution. On September 20th the Council of Ministers prepared a draft for a constitutional treaty and sent it to the King at Berg. The King's comment was: "This lucid and very thorough draft of a Federal treaty is in keeping with My intentions, with the exception of the provision according the Federal Head of State the right of personal inspection (in respect of the Bavarian army), which I am under no circumstances prepared to concede." This draft constitution was to be the basis for the negotiations in which the Bavarian plenipotentiaries were engaged in Versailles. When they departed on October 20th they were carrying a long list of the Bavarian Finance Minister's desiderata, such as the 30 millions war indemnity due from 1866, various exceptional items of war expenditure including compensation for the civilian

32

population of the Palatinate, and the Wittelsbachs' title to the Düsseldorf art gallery.

In addition, the King desired two million gulden for himself and a "modest increase of territory", as he repeatedly told Bray-Steinburg.[22] Territorial expansion and financial compensation were again the general theme of a letter written by the King to Prinz Luitpold on February 26th, 1871. In a letter of the same date to the Emperor William he mentions Bavaria's sacrifices in 1866. As such he describes the concessions "which in view of the status hitherto enjoyed by Bavaria can in truth only be called sacrifices". Bavaria, he continued, was the only existing State of the Confederation which, apart from a substantial sum of money, had lost "not inconsiderable territory. These losses were regarded by the majority of the population as a hardship and are even now a painful memory". The territorial enlargement sought for Bavaria would in particular reconcile those "who are all too ready to use the territorial losses of 1866 as a pretext for calling Prussia's pro-Confederation policy in question".

Payments to the Bavarian King and government
Ludwig II's cultural patronage

Bavaria was compensated, not territorially, but by the payment – by 1975 – of 157.9 million gulden; over a longer period the King received a total of 2 million gulden. The payments to the state did not commence until 1872, when Bismarck, entangled in his conflict with the Catholic Church, was increasingly dependent on Bavaria. Ludwig's share was paid as from 1873. Until the death of King Ludwig I in 1868 he had, like his father, received only half of the sum available from the Royal Civil List after deduction of expenses for the upkeep of the Court and the Court Theatre, as the other half of this figure – 500,000 gulden per annum – was reserved for King Ludwig I. It is hardly an accident that King Ludwig II waited until 1868 to begin building castles. The subsidies for Richard Wagner[23] (e.g., 1865: "Tristan" 70,000 gulden, 1866: "Lohengrin" and "Tannhäuser" 29,000 gulden, 1867: "Lohengrin" and "Tannhäuser"

44,000 gulden, 1868: "Meistersinger" 45,800 gulden, 1870 – "Walküre" 41,500 gulden), and now the cost of Neuschwanstein and Linderhof, not to speak of alterations to the Munich Residenz, seem soon, however, to have exceeded the King's resources, which were already sadly depleted by charitable commitments (average per annum 170,000 gulden, later 250–320,000 marks) and cultural projects (average per annum, 1866: 197,775 gulden, 1870: 287,579 gulden). This meant that by 1870 King Max II's private trust had also dwindled away to a negligible sum. It was in decisions on expenditure that Ludwig II first lost his sense of reality. The unusual way of raising money for his own purposes was admittedly a course that suggested itself in the autumn of 1870, as it was increasingly apparent that money was the only form of compensation still forthcoming for sacrifices in other sectors, but these financial demands prompted Bismarck in 1872 to appropriate these funds, which henceforth were normally made available through a clearing process with the Bavarian Finance Ministry, from the French war indemnity; it is true that the latter was drawn on by Prussia and – as from 1872 – by Württemberg. The payments made to Ludwig II as from 1873 were taken by Bismarck – no doubt without the knowledge of the recipient – from the forfeited treasury of the King of Hanover.

Castle projects

In 1867 the King travelled to Paris incognito, and in 1874 to Reims. Following his defeat in 1866, he was seeking a prototype in the Kings of France, of whom St. Louis and Louis XIV were his favoured precedents. The motivation for the castle of Neuschwanstein came from the Château Pierrefonds[24], built in 1392 by Louis of Orléans and restored between 1858 and 1895. Ludwig also derived inspiration from the Wartburg near Eisenach, which he visited in 1867, and especially from its Ministrels' Hall. He would evolve plans for different castles and palaces at the same time, and in some cases work was done on projects whose location was not yet determined. Dollmann's first plans for a palace such as was later realized on Herrenchiemsee date from 1868–1869, the site being given as "Linderhof". It was not until 1870 that the eighth – or "Versailles" – project dropped the reference to Linderhof – where, indeed, work had already been in progress since 1869 on a modest palace which was later to be the King's favourite residence.[25]

Ludwig's "Kaiserbrief" and attempts to form a Ministry with a stronger Bavarian image

Ludwig's famous letter offering the Imperial crown to the King of Prussia had no connection with the writer's financial wishes. It resulted from the agreements concluded by the Bavarian Ministers with Bismarck at Versailles on November 23rd, 1870. Just as in 1866 von der Pfordten, under the duress of the expiring armistice, had flouted the King's instructions by signing a peace treaty devoid of any guarantee for Bavarian sovereignty, so Count Bray-Steinburg did not always observe his King's wishes – for instance, when he ignored the latter in ending his co-operation with Württemberg, thus nullifying the démarche in Stuttgart on November 8th by the Bavarian Minister Baron von Gasser. Ludwig II was insisting on still greater Federal decentralization in the terms of the constitutional alliance, and objected in particular to the Federal Commander-in-Chief receiving the right to inspect Bavarian troops. Ludwig's view was that the greatest possible independence of Royal command over the Bavarian army was one of the essential components of Bavarian sovereignty.

Ludwig's confessor, Dr. Ludwig Trost, had already been endeavouring for some weeks to secure the King's consent to the foundation of the Empire – as had also one of his close associates already mentioned above, the philosophy Professor Dr. Johannes Huber, the text of whose lengthy memorandum on this subject is still extant. Ludwig himself had for some time been in favour of an Imperial solution, with the supreme office alternating between the Hohenzollerns and the Wittelsbachs and the Imperial capital between Berlin and Munich.

On November 30th, 1870 when Count Holnstein succeeded in reaching the King, who was confined to his bed at Hohenschwangau castle, Ludwig by no means transcribed the draft of the "Kaiserbrief" in the form submitted to him by Holnstein; he departed from Bismarck's formula by referring to the revival not only of the German Imperial title, but also of "a German Empire".[26] This evidently seemed to him more in the "general interest of the German Fatherland and its allied Princes" – a motive invoked more than once by Bismarck in his draft. In terms of greater solemnity than those used in the communication to King William of Prussia, Ludwig II suggested to the rulers of the individual German States that they join him in proposing to the King of Prussia that the tenure of the supreme office of the Confederation be combined with the title of German Emperor. In spite of these various communications drawn up on November 30th, 1870 Ludwig II was deeply affected – as also after the victory of Sédan – by the drastic change that would be entailed for the status of Bavaria and its King. The ruler who had written these letters at Hohenschwangau on November 30th was racked by doubts and desperation. To Cabinet Secretary August Eisenhart, who in his contacts with the King had frequently taken the part of the Ministers negotiating at Versailles, Ludwig wrote with some sarcasm that he (Eisenhart) had been amply enlightened by His (Ludwig's) Ministers en the German constitutional problem and was thus capable of grasping the situation. "Should, therefore, a communication in different terms (i.e. from those of Ludwig) prove better and more appropriate, should the sacrifices demanded of Me under the draft constitution be too great, the matter is then null and void, and I give you My authority to tear up the letter to the King of Prussia." It was the first time that the King had expressed himself to any other person in – politically speaking – such injudicious terms. Although he had given orders for his prompt identification with the national cause to be emphasized in the press, and had himself – by virtue of the immediate declaration of war on France – been successfully at pains to appear to Bismarck as a zealous ally – worthy, that is to say, of various rights and privileges – he was now seized by despair. Never (he wrote) had the waves of the Alpsee attracted him more as an element in which he might end his wretched existence. The notion that his proposal regarding the Imperial crown was not binding on his brother Otto made him wish to abdicate in the latter's favour. With great intelligence and exceptional self-control Ludwig II preserved his countenance towards his entourage, especially towards political personages. Inwardly, however, he sought more than once for ways and means of giving his Ministry a stronger Bavarian image[27] – in 1872, when he asked an intransigent Bavarian, Baron von Gasser, to form a government, and in 1875, when he tried to have a Ministry formed by Baron von und zu Franckenstein (one of the three objectors to the Versailles Treaties in the First Chamber) at the height of the "War in Sight" affair – at a highly critical moment for Bismarck's foreign policy. Gasser was defeated by his own blunders; Franckenstein declined office because he attached more importance to his leadership of the Centre Party in the Berlin Reichstag. The failure of both attempts to form a government on a more pronouncedly Bavarian basis was a severe blow for the King. When it became clear in 1876 that such attempts were simply not feasible – the decisive complication being the King's conflict with the Second Chamber and with the Bavarian Patriotic Party therein represented – the mood of despair gradually brought Ludwig's most dangerous symptoms to the surface.

King Ludwig II upholds his standpoint against Bismarck

Outwardly this development did not become noticeable for several years. He impressed Pius IX by the nobility of his reply (in 1873) to the Sovereign Pontiff's letter on Bismarck's anti-Catholic policy. Nor can we ignore the fact that instead of following the draft submitted by Lutz, his Minister of Education and Public Worship, the King had himself explained the legal difficulties and had patently avoided a breach.[28] On September 10th, 1879 Bismarck wrote the King an unusually long letter – a veritable treatise on the growing influence of Panslavism. He pointed out him the difficulties entailed on the one hand for the government of Tsar Alexander II, but on the other hand also for the German Empire and Austro-Hungary. To Ludwig Bismarck expounded a foreign policy plan. He had communicated it only to the Emperors William and Francis Joseph, but considered it his duty to acquaint the King of Bavaria "in all due respect ... with the policy of the German Empire". King Ludwig II, who was also informed of the secrecy of the plan as agreed upon with Count Andrassy, was thus bound to feel a figure in the European political scene. In accordance with Bismarck's request his consent was on the way by September 16[th.] Although we must not forget that Bismarck was endeavouring at the time to secure the dismissal of the Bavarian Foreign Minister, Baron von Pfretzschner, and the recall of the Bavarian Envoy in Berlin, Baron Gideon von Rudhart (both having displeased him by their outward insistence on Bavaria's status), it would be wrong to see in Bismarck's correspondence with King Ludwig II[29] solely the attempt – ultimately successful – to avoid convening the Foreign Affairs Committee of the Bundesrat, of which Bavaria had the chairmanship. Ludwig II did actually replace Pfretzschner with Baron Friedrich Krafft von Crailsheim, a Bavarian diplomat with German nationalist leanings who was not only young (born at Ansbach in 1841), but also the best candidate in the 1866 bar examinations, while Rudhart, who had been appointed in 1877 when Bismarck desired the recall of Baron Pergler von Perglas, was succeeded by Count Hugo von Lerchenfeld. It must be admitted that during this critical period Bismarck initiated King Ludwig his into policy and did at least attempt to secure his approval. There can be no doubt that in appointing Crailsheim Foreign Minister the King was deviating from the course pursued in 1872 and 1875 when he tried to install Ministries headed by Baron von Gasser and Baron von Franckenstein. In 1880, however, he did not name Crailsheim to preside over the Council of Ministers, although since its institution in 1849 this office had been combined with the Crown Affairs and Foreign portfolio. The King conferred the presidency of the Council of Ministers on a seasoned champion of Bavarian state authority, Baron von Lutz, who had been Minister of Justice (1867–1871) and was now Minister of Education and Public Worship (1869–1890). Along with Bray-Steinburg, the latter had made a signal contribution to the protection of Bavaria's rights and privileges (and those of other member States) under Article 78 of the Imperial Constitution, according to which the rights of a member State could not be modified against its will.

As late as 1883 and 1884, in after-dinner conversations with Ludwig at court, Franckenstein used to have the impression that the King's remarks were characterized by a "keen intelligence", and that no one could have seen in his utterances the slightest indication of any mental disturbance. This observation was committed to paper by Franckenstein in July 1886 – after the King had been declared insane, regency and guardianship had been proclaimed, and the disaster of June 13th had taken its course. Ludwig struggled valiantly, and in the end desperately, against his schizophrenic tendencies. They emerged increasingly, however, during the last decade of his life.

Götterdämmerung

Political disappointments
Human disappointments

This last decade began in 1876 with an auspicious event which made Ludwig happy – as had been the case back in 1864: in this year the Bayreuth Festival Theatre was completed. After eight years of separation the King celebrated a quiet reunion with Richard Wagner, whom he had not seen since his incognito visit to Switzerland. The population and the theatre audience gave the King a great ovation. The latter readied its climax when, after the performance of "Götterdämmerung", the King in his box and Wagner on the stage were to be seen simultaneously. Viewed in retrospect, the "Twilight of the Gods" strikes us as a theme fraught with gloomy premonitions. Inwardly the defeat of 1866, the inescapable participation in the foundation of the Empire, and the failure in 1872 and again in 1875 to form an administration with a stronger Bavarian image had been severe setbacks for the King's political consciousness. This made him all the more inclined to entertain exaggerated notions of his own Royal status. In addition, 1875 saw the irrevocable emergence of his brother's sickness. Ludwig wished his lack of contact with other people to be as inconspicuous as possible. He was disappointed by his subjective experiences with his own relatives and with persons belonging to the upper classes of society. On the other hand the King, who had intellectual pretensions and read a great deal as a result of his solitary way of life,[30] was conscious of an educational disparity in conversation with an officer of his entourage or with his servants. It was not as though Ludwig disliked contacts with men and women of humble origin; nor did his sense of dynastic priority by any means call for his immediate associates to be drawn preferably from the established nobility. He appreciated high society, as exemplified by opera audiences, so little that he preferred private performances. These took place in the normal evening hours, and by no means only after midnight. Between Ludwig and servants – as well as the members of the Light Horse in attendance on him – there was normally a

41

gulf determined by their function. With a few, however, the lonely ruler was on familiar terms; indeed, a regular friendship existed between him and his equerry Richard Hornig (b. 1841). Ludwig's male attachments should on no account be assessed as proof of his schizophrenia; the individual cases are hardly to be substantiated. His incessant attempts to justify his actions in theological terms[31] would seem to prohibit imaginative speculations in this field. A genuine relationship of loyalty and confidence prevailed between the King and his adjutant, Count Alfred von Dürckheim-Montmartin. He was Ludwig's junior by five years, had augmented his education by reading languages for three semesters at Munich University before taking his commission, had served through the 1870–1871 war and had passed out of a military academy with General Staff qualifications. As adjutant to Prince Arnulf, who represented Bavaria during the Russo-Turkish war of 1878–1879 in the capacity of observer, he had witnessed this campaign, and in 1881 had married the daughter of the Russian Court Chamberlin, Count Bobrinsky. The marriage, of which one daughter was born, ended in separation in 1885; Dürkheim, who was Ludwig's ADC as from 1883, disclosed his troubles to the King and served him with great personal devotion.

Ludwig's mental and moral schizophrenia

Most of the King's friendships, such as those with Baron Anton von Hirschberg or the actor Joseph Kainz, broke up after some time when differences of opinion revealed great disparities of character. Kainz, whom the King forgave for falling asleep during their protracted conversations, told him that he could see nothing noble in using his position to treat servants with a lack of consideration and kindness. Even if the latter did not always deserve Kainz's sympathy – they frequently cheated the King and lied to him – Ludwig had such poor control over his eccentric notions of absolute authority that he occasionally boxed their ears or spat in their faces. In the last few years of the King's life his outbreaks of anger betrayed nothing less than a split personality. Whereas in the normal state he was generous,

kind, and largely free of prejudices, an attempt to overcome the financial
and other limitations of his actual power might lead him to give orders for
atrocities or a bank robbery outside Bavaria. The non-fulfilment of such
commands never resulted in particular difficulties. It is typical, however,
of the King's changeable state towards the end of his life that he never
referred again to the execution of such orders.

This was an acknowledgement of the exceptional state in which they had
been given.

After Lorenz von Düfflipp relinquished the post of Court Secretary in
1877, the management of the Cabinet Fund became increasingly chaotic.
Ludwig's increasing aloofness assumed the form of persecution mania.[32]
His unfounded fear of assassination was the very antithesis of his highly
unrealistic conception of a sublime absolute monarchy in the style of Louis
XIV. Though not selfish, he seemed to see himself as the focal point of the
outside world. This led to the politically impossible situation in which he
occasionally denied that laws were binding on him individually; once he
told Düfflipp that the King's word was valid only so long as he chose to
keep it.

Prince Luitpold and the Ministry intervene
Ludwig's attempts to salvage his Cabinet Fund reveal abnormal notions
of authority

Prince Luitpold, the kinsman next to Otto in the line of succession, whom
the King almost invariably called upon to take his place at openings of
Parliament, in the Council of State and at State visits, sent in summer
1885 for the President of the Council of Ministers, Baron von Lutz, and
asked him whether the Ministers raised no objections to conduct on the
King's part that was calculated to be so deleterious for the dynasty and the
country.[33] Upon this, Lutz called the Council of Ministers, who took the
view that some such step might make an impression on the King, but
feared that the result might be the necessity of their resignation. It was not
denied that they had a certain moral responsibility and duty in this mat-

ter. The Council of Ministers considered that the first move should come from members of the Royal Family. Prince Luitpold expressed his willingness, and merely wished to receive a hint regarding the suitable moment. Things began to move on August 29th, when the King himself ordered Finance Minister Emil von Riedel to take the necessary steps "to improve the financial situation" – a reference to the "unsatisfactory state" of the Cabinet Fund mentioned in the foregoing sentence.[34] The necessary steps were also expected to promote the King's "projects". On September 3rd the Minister replied, after consulting the Ministry at large, that the state of the Cabinet Fund represented a great danger for the person of the King and for the Monarchy, and could be remedied only by economies and retrenchment. The King reacted by ordering his Adjutant-General to inform Riedel of his displeasure, upon which the latter tendered his resignation. The other Ministers declared that following Riedel's dismissal they would not be in a position to continue their functions, upon which the King declined Riedel's resignation in the most flattering terms possible, but instructed the Adjutant-General to convey his displeasure to the Ministers jointly and severally, and described it as *lèse-majesté* for the Ministers to tender their resignation because he, Ludwig, chose to dismiss one of their number. Shortly after Christmas he sent a messenger to the President of the Council of Ministers with the order to state what, in his view, ought to be done about the current state of the Cabinet Fund. Mindful of Riedel's experiences, Lutz did not venture to submit a report to the King direct, but sent the Court Secretary an involved disquisition expressing his gratitude for the confidence reposed in him by the King for twenty-one years; he then sought with the utmost circumspection to prove that it could not be a matter of *lèse-majesté* when Ministers were unwilling to drop one of their number who had been censured in this manner. There followed warning – on behalf of the other Ministers – not to approach the Landtag for a sum over and above the Civil List, as the Ministers would not be able to assume responsibility for such a request to the two Chambers. Lutz gave an even more dismal account of the Cabinet Fund than Riedel, and then alluded to the possibility of attachment proceedings being instituted in respect of the King's estate, and of the same possibly being productive of a dangerous solidarity among the creditors. In point of fact there was no provision to prevent the King from applying to the two Chambers for any given sum. Inclusive of the next instalment of the building costs, the King required 20 millions, which, as against a budget of 300 million marks, was no unattainable figure. Ludwig did not reply to Lutz, but made enquiries of the Minister of the Interior, von Feilitzsch, about a new Court Secretary, and desired to know whether the castles which were the King's private property could not be transferred for form's sake to the Civil List schedule and thus be safeguarded against seizure. On January 19th, 1886 the Minister of the Interior answered in the negative. Then, on January 26th, the King entreated him at least to raise the sum necessary "to prevent an encroachment on Royal property – for if this could not be averted My indignation would be such that I should either take My life or else depart at once and for ever from the ill-favoured country where this disgrace occurred. There are surely faithful subjects capable of preventing this." Since the state of the Cabinet Fund had deteriorated, the King went on, there had been delays in the construction which had "robbed him of life's chief satisfaction". Understandable though Ludwig's entreaty was in human terms, the threat of self-destruction was quite preposterous. The Minister of the Interior stated that the 20 millions could not be raised and that an appeal to the parliamentary organs would be futile. The use by his grandfather, King Ludwig I, of unexpended public funds for architectural projects had provoked a constitutional crisis which led to the agreement of July 12th, 1843. This laid down that the government was not entitled to appropriate surplus items without consulting the Landtag. The King was urged to seek a compromise with his creditors on the basis of a reduction of excessive claims, and to practise economy. While the King was vainly attempting to secure a loan from Rothschild in Paris, but also in Berlin, Brussels, Stockholm and elsewhere, Lutz was already conferring with Prince Luitpold on the necessity of a regency and discussing the King's mental state. The Ministry was also in touch with Berlin. But the King, too, was not idle. First he made an indirect approach to Franckenstein through Prince Ludwig Ferdinand, and then on April 15th he despatched Cabinet Secretary von Schneider to him to enquire what advice Francken-stein had for the King. Franckenstein considered an application to the two Chambers impossible. Were it to be submitted by the Ministers, this would entail a solemn undertaking by the King to refrain in future from expenditure in excess of his revenue. At the request of von Lutz, Franckenstein discussed the situation with him, Feilitzsch and Crailsheim. Franckenstein asserted that the King was not mentally deranged. What was regarded as abnormal, he said, was an imagination of infinite sensitivity which had never encountered resistance – a fact for which the Ministers shared the blame. Lutz replied that Dr. Gudden, the alienist, considered the King "definitely crazy". The King continued to correspond through Schneider with Franckenstein, who urged him to come to Munich and discuss the situation with his Ministry. In the event of the King not doing so he, Franckenstein, could only advise him to summon the President of the Council of Ministers, Baron von Lutz. In this desperate situation Ludwig also made an approach to Bismarck, who advised him on April 14th to raise a State loan and to concern himself personally with affairs in Munich.

Ludwig under guardianship; Luitpold Regent

On May 5th the Ministry addressed a joint remonstrance to the King, criticized his financial arrangements even more frankly and called for economy and retrenchment. The King failed to reply. The press, however, was already speculating about whether the King could be taken to court for private liabilities, and decided that he could. Foreign papers were criticizing the King without restraint.

At this juncture Prince Luitpold, by virtue of a paper already drawn up by Crailsheim on May 2nd, requested Friedrich von Ziegler, who on February 11th, 1872 had become legal assistant in Ludwig's Cabinet, where he had served as the King's secretary from January 1st, 1877 until November 11th, 1879, and his successor (until May 19th, 1880) Ludwig August Müller (von Müller as from 1891), who had studied law in Munich and Berlin from 1865 to 1869, to furnish facts for a psychiatric report on the King. With Ziegler's dismissal in 1879 personal audiences with the King in connection with State business had ceased altogether. As from June 4th the

Chief Equerry, Count Maximilian von Holnstein, was expected to instruct his subordinates – that is to say, Ludwig's servants – to report their observations. The medical report of June 8th, drawn up by four neurologists of repute, including Gudden and Grashey, declared the King to be "in an advanced state of mental disintegration", insane, "incurable" and incapacitated for life for the exercise of his Royal duties. Luitpold summoned the Ministers to a meeting at 11 a.m. on June 7th. The proceedings began without the President of the Council of Ministers and Minister of Education and Public Worship, Baron von Lutz, the other Ministers stated that the King had not seen fit to respond to their joint remonstrance of May 5th; feeling, therefore, incapable of further constructive conduct of government business, they wished to tender their resignation. Should, however, the physicians find Ludwig permanently incapacitated for the discharge of State affairs, the "expedient of resignation" was out of the question, and it was their "bounden duty" to take constitutional steps for the establishment of a regency. The Finance Minister expressed the view that a compromise with the creditors, of whom not a few had "succumbed to the temptation to overcharge", would be rendered very difficult, if not impossible, by any proposal in the Landtag. He advised against this course. Crailsheim demonstrated by citing a number of occurrences in recent years to what extent – precisely in his departments of Crown and Foreign Affairs – an "increasing pathological abstinence from State duties and from the exercise of important Royal functions" had been making itself felt. At this stage Chief Minister von Lutz arrived in the company of the chief medical adviser, Dr. von Gudden. Luitpold asked the latter for a statement. On the basis of the data communicated to him, and with repeated references to the pathological mental state of Ludwig's brother Otto, Gudden described the King as incapacitated by virtue of a serious mental disturbance. Personal examination and observation he held to be neither admissible nor feasible so long as the Crown functions were vested in the King. The documents, however, left no room for doubt. Ludwig's protestations of disillusionment and distaste for life in general prompted Gudden to fear a suicide attempt, which, he said, must be averted, as must also a possible escape bid. On June 13th this conclusion was to cost Gudden his life.

47

Lutz did not attach very great importance to the accounts of Ludwig cited by Gudden, which were bound under the circumstances to be extremely superficial, but expected more from the meeting envisaged at Hohenschwangau and from the delivery to Ludwig of a letter from Luitpold regarding the necessity for the establishment of a regency. Crailsheim read out the draft of Luitpold's letter to his Royal nephew, and the Minister of the Interior that of a proclamation by Luitpold concerning the assumption of the regency and the convening of the Landtag on June 15th. The Minister of War proposed an appropriate order of the day to the Bavarian army. One day before the proclamation the governments of friendly states were to be notified of the step decided upon.

At a meeting on June 8th, Luitpold decided first that all members of the Royal Family in the line of succession were to be notified of the Regency, and then approved the Ministers' drafts from the previous day. The Minister of the Interior was requested to draft a message to the two Chambers of the Landtag. A noon on June 9th, at Luitpold's request, Chief Minister Dr. von Lutz read out the report of the four medical consultants (Gudden, Hagen, Grashey and Hubrich) and the depositions therein adduced.

On this subject Luitpold wrote to his Royal nephew the same day to the effect that his "present" state of health, as ascertained by a number of medical consultants, was prejudicial to the exercise of his State functions. For this reason, and in consideration of the all too patent incapacity of Prince Otto, it was his (Luitpold's) sad duty to introduce measures for the constitutional establishment of a regency. Having convened an immediate session of the Landtag, he had "assumed provisional control of the government" and had appointed Chief Equerry Count Maximilian von Holnstein and Count Clemens von Toerring-Jettenbach (a member of the First Chamber) to be trustees in charge of Ludwig's personal and individual affairs. Of this Luitpold notified the King "with all respect and humility", praying that God might grant Ludwig the strength to bear with Royal dignity the inexorable consequences of the grave infirmity that the Almighty had visited upon him. Luitpold also prayed, however, that "God in His infinite wisdom" might grant "an early recovery as a prerequisite for the rescission" of these measures essential in Ludwig's own interest. In this hope he remained "in unyielding affection and loyalty to Your Royal and August Person, Your most excellent Majesty's humble and obedient subject and uncle, Prince Luitpold". Luitpold went to the length of modifying the medical report by mentioning that "in all probability" Ludwig's complaint would last for life, but on the same day (June 9th), as the potential regent next in the line of succession, requested the "Ministers on the strength of the medical report to take a final decision under Art. II, Par. 11 of the constitution, i.e. on the establishment of a regency. The response of the Ministers was that the conditions for the establishment of a regency, and the assumption of this office by Luitpold, were fulfilled. The latter now put his signature to the proclamation submitted on June 7th and adopted on the 8th, as well as to the writ summoning the two Chambers. The Ministers adopted a proposal by Lutz that a committee from each Chamber should be appointed for the "previous examination" of the matter, to the members of which the evidence was to be made available. The public were to be excluded from the sessions of these committees and of the Chambers. To the Bavarian army, of which Luitpold had Inspector-General since 1869, he himself issued the order of the day proposed by the War Minister.

Luitpold notified the Rulers within the German Empire and the Emperor of Austria, and on June 10th proclaimed the regency. The Landtag was summoned for June 15th.

Ludwig's desperate struggle

At the very beginning of June Ludwig wished to make a further approach to Bismarck – not knowing that the latter had already been notified by the Munich authorities. On June 3rd, 1886, however, having already received adverse intelligence from Munich, he wrote to Hesselschwerdt, a stable official who possessed his confidence: "… to send someone reliable to Bismarck. It is disgraceful for the Chambers, the Ministers and Schneider (the Cabinet Secretary) to mention such impertinent conditions. So make short shrift of the Chamber. If it remains obstinate – as it seems in view of its unforeseeably atrocious conduct – dissolve it and install another. Quick

49

action is needed, for there is no time to lose. Mark My words." Hesselschwerdt from the stable personnel and Hoppe, a hairdresser, were expected to take measures for the formation of a new Ministry by the former Cabinet Secretary, Friedrich von Ziegler, and Friedrich J. von Thelemann, a lawyer who was engaged to the daughter of the then Minister of Justice, Fäustle, and himself held the justice portfolio years later. On May 19th Ziegler had made the last attempt to secure the King's co-operation. Ludwig neither yielded nor followed the advice of Bismarck and Franckenstein to show himself in Munich and to discharge his duties there. On June 9th he issued a proclamation "to my beloved Bavarian subjects and to the entire German Nation" and also addressed himself to the German Emperor, accusing Luitpold and the Ministry of treason. Dürckheim was responsible for its despatch to a number of newspaper offices, but it was published only by one Russian journal and by one in Bamberg. Among other recipients, it reached Ludwig's cousin, Prince Leopold, in the Schwabinger Landstrasse, Munich, as well as Crailsheim, Lutz and Holnstein via Bâle, being postmarked June 12th. Prince Luitpold had written his nephew the critical letter in which he sought to explain the situation in human terms. Instead of sending it to him by post, however, he had it delivered by an official deputation. The fact that this included Count Holnstein (contrary to the admonitions of Bismarck, who knew that he had a strong dislike of the King for the last three years), incensed Ludwig to such a degree that in the early morning of June 10th – the day on which his uncle proclaimed the regency in Munich, he ordered the arrest of the entire deputation, including Crailsheim and Holnstein. For the treatment of the detained officials he gave orders whose very cruelty aroused doubts in the minds of the responsible staff. They released their prisoners – no doubt without the King's knowledge. Leopold Hitzl (son of the fire-brigade chief Lukas Hitzl) even claims that they were freed by order of the King.

The facts, as reported by Crailsheim, are that at 2 p.m. the District Commissioner from Füssen induced the police to release the deputation. The King had succeeded in apprehending the deputation mainly because he had sent a mounted policeman named Brückner to Füssen with instructions to Police-Sergeant Boppeler to appear with his entire unit, and because this official carried out his King's orders in defiance even of top-ranking Court dignitaries and Ministers such as Holnstein and Crailsheim. Ludwig II had also caused Bruckner to summon the Füssen Commissioner immediately, informing him that a *coup d'état* was in progress. Whereas the sergeant at once reported to the King, the administrative chief chose to await developments in the hostelry "Zur Alpenrose". According to Boppeler's report, written on June 20th, 1886 and conveyed to Ludwig's brother Otto, he was told that the deputation had arrived to place Ludwig II under restraint and to remove him from the place; Luitpold was intending to usurp the throne. "To be deposed causes me no pain, but to be buried alive on grounds of insanity, to be belaboured by warders' fists like my brother Otto – this I cannot bear! I am less than a beggar, who can at least invoke the courts; this, as King, I cannot." Dürckheim and Boppeler advised Ludwig to make his way via the Tyrol (whither the route could not yet be closed) to Munich, and to summon the Landtag forthwith. Ludwig acknowledged that this was "the simplest way", but failed to act accordingly, his objection being: "We are not living in an age of Might before Right; I shall make use of my rights and shall not leave; My subjects shall judge whether I am crazy or not." At the time a popular verdict of this kind would probably have been very much in the King's favour. The attitude of the population backed up the sergeant from Füssen in the execution of the orders, and literally invested him with authority as against the deputation, whose members were terrified of the excited crowds. Although Gudden threatened that the sergeant's conduct might cost him his head, as the King was out of his mind and in no position to give orders, Boppeler denied all knowledge of this, and declared that he would execute his order even if he had to use violence. Gudden now pointed out that he was not the head of the deputation, and referred him to Crailsheim. The latter, at first furious, then resorted to all manner of promises: Boppeler was to tell His Majesty that he had not found the persons he was to arrest. "We will disappear singly and inconspicuously." The sergeant, however, refused "I'm not a soldier that breaks his oath; I've sworn allegiance and am not going back on my word."

The same morning Ludwig tried to send telegrams to the German Emperor, William I, and to the Emperor Francis Joseph, but also to the commanders of various regiments. The responsible postal official, who had already received instruction from the Department of Posts and Communications in Munich consigned them to the waste-paper basket, from where – but not until later – Boppeler recovered them. The telegram despatched to the Imperial Chancellor by Ludwig's adjutant, Count Dürckheim, on June 10th did actually reach its destination. A crowd "numbering about a thousand" maligned the arrested deputation when they were marched off, as a "gang of scoundrels and regicides, traitors, usurpers and oath-breaking villains" Boppeler, assisted by the chief of the fire brigade (also summoned by the King), prevented violence. On the strength of Boppeler's report, Ludwig gave orders for each of the prisoners to be confined in a separate room, to be divested of his uniform and kept under strict surveillance. The result was that Crailsheim could not deliver Luitpold's letter of June 9th to the King. He was, however, unwilling – as he himself reported to Luitpold on June 11th – to have it conveyed to the King (possibly by Boppeler) in the presence of Count Dürckheim. As he had been concerned with the final version of this communication, he knew its purport. Ludwig was to die in ignorance of the letter.

Following the arrest of the deputation – according to Boppeler – Ludwig gave orders "to harness the horses. He would proceed to Munich and show himself to the population". Count Dürckheim then came in and advised against this course. The proclamation of the regency had been made public. The King would no longer be able to pass in safety. He would be seized and confined in an institution – for which all preparations had been made. It is a fact that on this very day (June 10th) the regency was already proclaimed and the Director-General of the Posts and Communications Department, von Hochede appropriately briefed by Crailsheim. While the next step was under consideration a police detachment of 36 men arrived from Munich and sealed off all entrances to the castle.

When Ludwig saw the Munich police formation, he turned to Boppeler, who by Royal authority was in command of all personnel from Füssen, and said: "Here I am – a prisoner, without committing any crime". He naturally considered himself in the right in having ordered the arrest of the deputation by the sergeant from Füssen – especially as he was unaware of the existence of Luitpold's letter of June 9th. "What have I done to my subjects to be forsaken like this? Wretched King that I am, have I no friend to help me?" In Boppeler's presence Ludwig II took counsel with Dürckheim about what was to be done. One point was the possibility of escape – but by now all routes were blocked. Count Dürckkeim "saw to some papers" and the King burnt letters from Hesselschwerdt and others so that no one should be compromised "for His sake".

The Bavarian Minister of War, Adolph Heinleth, who had been appointed by Ludwig II as recently as April 16th, 1885, had served in 1870–71 as Chief of Staff of the Bavarian 1st Army Corps, and had been Chief of Staff of the whole Bavarian Army since 1878, now sent two telegrams – the second of them already citing Luitpold's authority – ordering Dürckheim to proceed to Munich at once. As Minister of War Heinleth was also Judge-Advocate General of the Army. When Dürckheim showed second telegram to the King, the latter said: "You know much I should like to keep you with me; send my uncle (Luitpold) a telegram to ask if he will leave you in my service". Ludwig's acknowledgement of such a decision by Prince Luitpold was tantamount to an abdication. Although the second telegram (at Crailsheim's behest) warned the Count that insubordination would be regarded as high treason, Dürckheim sought confirmation in Munich. When the order from the War Ministry was reiterated, Ludwig said to his faithful adjutant: "I realize that you have to return, otherwise you will forfeit your entire career and prospects".

Boppeler spent the night of June 10th to the 11th at the castle. At 9 a.m., when a supply van entered the courtyard and an institution warder alighted, the sergeant hurried down and enquired about the contents of the vehicle, but was not answered. Looking inside, he discovered a bottle of chloroform, which he smashed on the flagstones with the remark: "Someone wants to send us all to sleep." When he reported the occurrence, the King, deathly pale, wrung his hands and moaned: "How wretched I am compared with you. I have not a soul to share my suffering. If only it were all over! To Boppeler Ludwig seemed to be preoccupied with death.

On June 11th, too, the regency proclamation reached Hohenschwangau. Durckheim, who had given advance notice of his arrival in Munich, was apprehended, but very soon released again; at 11:47 p.m. on June 15th he left for Elbigenalp to join the Queen Mother.

Ludwig's last days

Hardly a soul was left at Neuschwanstein, and Ludwig was awaiting the fate that had overtaken his brother. As so often before on his departure from the Munich Residenz, and from the throne in particular, he paced through the castle that embodied so many of his ideas and took leave of the splendid, but uncompleted, Throne Room with its portraits of Royal Saints.

The King, who had eaten nothing for two days, told his footman Lorenz Mayr in the course of the day that he wished to dine in the Minstrels' room at 6 p.m. Meanwhile the District Medical Officer, Dr. Pöpf, arrived in response to the King's summons. Ludwig asked him "whether he thought him crazy, as others seemed to". The doctor replied rather gruffly, according to Boppeler's account, but evidently with great psychological insight: "In that case we are all crazy; I have been in practice for many years and have rarely come across anyone completely normal." "It seems", replied the King, "that I am no crazier than other people." He dismissed the doctor courteously.

During the night – it rained in torrents – he talked to 24-year-old Alfons Weber, hitherto of the Light Horse, who was detailed for the first spell of personal attendance: "Do you believe in the immortality of the soul, in Life Hereafter and retribution?" – "Yes, Your Majesty." – The King: "So do I, although I have read a number of books that were very confusing – but there must be retribution; what they are doing to me cannot go unpunished!" Then, obviously incensed: "I can endure being robbed of my throne, but I shall not survive being declared insane. Let my fate be visited upon those who have betrayed and destroyed me." He gave Weber the diamond brooch that he used to wear on his hat and all the money he had in his desk: "Take it, take it, I need no money any more." Although not a drinker, he helped himself to wine and brandy indiscriminately in the dining-room – as if to numb himself: "I was born at half-past twelve, and at half-past twelve I should like to die." He handed Weber a small, well-worn prayer-book opened at the prayers for the dying, and said: "Pray for me!" From footman Mayr, who, on being questioned without the King's previous knowledge, had given evidence to his prejudice, he requested the key to the tower – no doubt to plunge to his destruction – but in vain.

55

Dr. Bernhard von Gudden

When the King – possibly somewhat later than the time he had appointed – was about to seat himself for dinner, Boppeler opened the double doors. On stepping forward, Ludwig saw that strangers were coming up the stairs. He asked Boppeler to see who they were, and the latter recognized the four (or three?) warders. Before he could report this fact, he found the King face to face with Dr. von Gudden and his assistant Dr. Franz Karl Müller, who had been in attendance on Prince Otto since December 1st. On their arrival at Neuschwanstein "towards midnight", as noted by Dr. Müller, but at all events in the late evening, the footman Lorenz Mayr had implored Dr. von Gudden to come to the King's apartments, as His Majesty was very excited and, having failed to obtain the key to the tower, might now throw himself out the window. Gudden had his men mount guard on the entrance to the tower and told Mayr to give the King the key he had asked for. The King appeared in the door to the corridor, and the warders grasped him by the arms. Dr. Gudden disclosed to him that his condition had been reported on by four alienists, on the strength of which Prince Luitpold had assumed the regency. He had orders to take the King to Schloss Berg the very same night. The King groaned once or twice: "Oh dear!", "What's the meaning of all this?", but very soon recovered his extraordinary self-composure, suffered the doctors and warders to be introduced to him, and carried on several conversations before it was time to depart – just after daybreak. He even asked who was now to assume the regency, although he knew the answer very well. When Gudden named the King's uncle, Ludwig remarked in a not unfriendly, but somewhat patronizing tone: "Well, well, good old Luitpold" – although in the last 48 hours he had repeatedly called him the Rebel Prince. Indeed, at Berg he told Gudden that he was a man of honour, but weak in character, who had been misused by the party behind the conspirators. Were such remarks by Ludwig "soft soap" for Gudden – he himself occasionally described such subterfuges in similar terms? At Neuschwanstein Ludwig had enquired about various details in the treatment of his brother, whom, in spite of the protest letter against his confinement in Nymphenburg Palace, he held very dear, repeatedly visited, and often calmed down after outbreaks of fury by the psychological deployment of Royal authority. Then, however, Ludwig had suddenly turned on Gudden: "How can you certify me insane without seeing me and examining me beforehand?" Gudden in turn cited the "overwhelming" documentary evidence, thus provoking the sick ruler, whom the whole situation had rendered extremely irritable, in a manner betraying indifferent psychological acumen. Boppeler states that Gudden had commenced the encounter with Ludwig as follows: "Your Majesty is suffering from a complaint that necessitates examination", upon which Ludwig strode to and fro with his arms folded, eyed Gudden piercingly for some time, and then asked: "Listen, as an experienced neurologist, how can you be so devoid of scruple as to make out a certificate that is decisive for a human life? You have not seen me for the last 12 years! "Gudden, "in some confusion": "I took this step on the strength of the evidence." Ludwig: "Ah, on the strength of the evidence of these paid lackeys that I have raised from nothing, and they betray me in return! And how long, assuming that I am really sick, do you think my cure will take?" Gudden: "That will depend upon Your Majesty; it will be necessary for Your Majesty to submit to my instructions". The King (quite incensed): "No Wittelsbach – let me tell you once and for all – need ever submit to anything!" He refused food, but not even hard words scared away the doctors. He walked "back and forth all night amid wails and groans, from time to time" calling Boppeler by name and imploring him not to desert him. The works of

Gottfried von Böhm and Werner Richter, though otherwise informative, fail to mention Boppeler – unlike that of Rupert Hacker. At about four in the morning Ludwig II said: "Sergeant! I thank you and your men for the faithful service you have rendered me; I am most truly sorry that I cannot reward you; go your way with my blessing – we shall not meet again." To one Niggl, of the castle staff, he said: "Preserve these rooms as a sacred precinct, and let no curious eyes profane them!" He referred to rooms "in which I have spent the bitterest hours of my life. Farewell! They will not see me again." Before the departure the King had a long conversation with Mayr, who was to procure him potassium cyanide. On the castle steps, where two officers senior to Boppeler had taken up their position, he turned round once more: "Farewell, Schwanstein, child of my sorrows!" A Major who approached him was looked up and down "quite contempt-uously", and told: "Don't put your hands on me, I can go alone. When the carriage left Schwanstein" – Boppeler's account – "a crowd of over three thousand had gathered, there was shouting and weeping, the King waved acknowledgement in all directions and pressed the hands of children who threw flowers into the carriage. I (Boppeler) shall never forget this funeral procession for a living ruler." Police Superintendent Horn, on the other hand, puts the number of the spectators at about 20. The discrepancy between the two statements in naturally prejudicial to the credibility of both. At Seeshaupt, where there was a change of horses, the King thanked a landlord's wife three times for the glass of water he had requested – only one of many encounters of which the story is told to this day.

After arriving at Schloss Berg the King again displayed exceptional self-control. Gudden was positively delighted with Ludwig's courtesy. The first walk passed off without incident – although the King did detect two uniformed figures in the undergrowth and enquired, not without irony, whether such precautions were actuated by the proximity of Socialists. This induced Gudden to have the policemen withdrawn. The King, who had had the latest report on Otto's sickness on his desk at Neuschwanstein immediately before his enforced departure, now voiced objections to a guardianship based on imputed mental incapacity and attributed every-thing "to the (non-existent) craving for power on the part of the Prince

Regent".[35] His persecution complex grew with the discovery of peep-holes in the doors at Schloss Berg – as well as other "facilities". Even attendance at divine service was refused him on Whit Sunday, June 13th. After his evening meal on this day the King sent for Gudden to accompany him on a second walk that had been promised him. The doctor dismissed an attendant who had been detailed to escort them. This was the evening on which the King and Dr. Gudden lost their lives in the Starnberger See. According to the post-mortem examination the King's body displayed no external injuries apart from a slight knee abrasion; the pathological findings, however, revealed advanced tissue degeneration affecting the cranium, the cerebrum and the meninges. This was attributed to abnormal development, but also to chronic inflammation, both recent and of long standing. Abdominal distension set in while the body was still at Berg. One of the surgical measures was the removal of the heart, which the King, like many of the Wittelsbachs, had destined for the Chapel of Grace at Altötting. The official record does not specify the cause of death, and to this day there is no convincing proof for any of the theories advanced. Although Ludwig had spoken of the wish to end his life, it would have been extremely difficult for a good swimmer – and such he was – to carry this out in view of the automatic reaction of a powerful physique. The suicide theory is rivalled by other conjectures. One of these assumes an attempt on the part of the King to escape to a waiting vehicle by water instead of along the obstructed lakeside route. Gudden is supposed to have stood in his way; the King overpowered him, but succumbed to a stroke in the icy water.

When the dead King was lying in state at Schloss Berg, one of those performing a vigil of several hours was Martin Beck, the parish priest of Aufkirchen. As the incumbent of a lakeside living he had frequently seen bodies recovered from the waves, but Ludwig's features convinced him that "this man had not been drowned". He also knew that Gudden had reassured his own parents by writing that he "always had the wherewithal about him to overcome the King, although he was his physical superior". Does this mean that Gudden attempted to narcotise Ludwig before or during their struggle? That the King collapsed for this reason after a number of paces parallel to the shore? Do possible circumstances such as this modify our speculations as to the intentions of the King when he walked into the lake? An additional fact is that all present-day medical enquiry must transpose the mode of expression used at the time by Ludwig's doctors into modern parlance, not to speak of the allowance to be made for the grave suspicion evinced by Ludwig against them in 1886.

The shocking report drawn up by the four neurologists on June 8th, which tells of the progressive disintegration of Ludwig's command of his intellectual powers, makes use of evidence given by the equerry Richard Hornig, who had served the King since 1867 and had attained a close human relationship with him: "His Majesty was considering whether, in return for a substantial sum, he might make over the kingdom to His Royal Highness Prince Luitpold, or sell it to Prussia."[36] Such unorthodox – and no doubt late – products of Ludwig's ingenuity, however, were never realized. On the other hand, the members of the 1886 deputation, who were intended to form an idea of his complaint and its consequences, were anything but equal to the exceptional intelligence, self-control and historic faculties of a patient obsessed with his kingly destiny. If he had had a sight of Luitpold's letter of June 9th, its references to the hope of recovery and to a limited duration of the regency might have allayed the mental tempest in the unfortunate ruler. The experiences of the past days, the enforced departure from Neuschwanstein, and Gudden's vacillation between extremes in the therapy applied at Schloss Berg all impelled Ludwig to a course that will in all probability never permit of ultimate elucidation, but which ended in his death. On the morning of June 14th, Prince Regent Luitpold exclaimed with tears in his eyes: "I shall be called his murderer".[37] Of no one was this less true than of this uncle, who in 1870–1871 – politically the most difficult episode of his nephew's reign – had been his closest associate in State affairs.

Even some days before the cataclysm, notable manifestations of loyalty and devotion were reaching the King from wide sections of the population. A letter written by a "true Bavarian" in time to get to the King personally closed with the verdict: "Anyone who thinks differently is a regicide and a Prussian spy." After the disaster of June 13th this attitude engendered rumours to the effect that Ludwig had been murdered. They are at variance not only with the report on the post-mortem examination, but also with the depositions of the police officers on duty, whose guns were unloaded.

Ludwig used occasionally to mention a wish to remain an enigma to others. He certainly presented one to his brother and, finally, to himself. On the strength of reports by Otto's physicians, Ludwig wrote to him on January 23rd, 1872 that since no improvements in his state of health had take place in the course of the last few weeks, he was compelled in grave concern to endorse the views of the medical advisers with regard to the indispensable necessity of thorough therapeutical measures. He was to take up residence with his usual suite and with the Court physician, Dr. Brattler, at Nymphenburg Palace and to comply at all times with the instructions of the doctors in respect of his personal mode of life and of the rules of the establishment. He (Ludwig) had invested them with the necessary authority. This was his Royal will. He nevertheless assured him of his sincere fraternal sympathy and affection and implored the aid of the Almighty. On March 4th, 1872, Otto replied with a heart-rending protest. For 400 years no Prince of "our family" had been treated thus. Otto's allusion was to Duke Caspar of Zweibrücken, who on December 20th, 1490 was imprisoned on grounds of alleged insanity by his co-reigning younger brother Alexander, and died at Nohfelden castle on the Nahe (near Saarbrücken) in 1527, when Alexander's son Ludwig II was already on the throne in Zweibrücken. In point of fact Caspar's conduct was so singular that his father intended, in the event of his wife surviving him, that she should decide with which of the sons not in holy orders she wished to reign pending his majority. Caspar is known to have occasionally offered armed resistance to his father.

Otto wrote to Ludwig that in the quarters he had hitherto occupied he had been attacked late in the evening "by two individuals", forced "immediately" to rise from his bed, where, all unsuspecting, he had been lying peacefully, compelled to dress and, although he had not been out of doors for weeks, "dragged" in the pouring rain to Nymphenburg in a carriage, there to be welcomed "like a laughing-stock" by liveried persons with lighted flambeaux (tall branched candlesticks). He could not admit to any offence; his conscience was clean. He had invariably had a dislike for journeys whose destination was Munich. He would never forget that Ludwig was the "initiator of this treatment". "You have no right to order me to proceed to this or to that place within the Kingdom; you have no right, seeing that I have done no wrong, to treat me thus." Otto protested: "I have submitted to duress, and am a prisoner; my treatment has been disgraceful!" ... "I am now your prisoner unless and until you choose to set me at liberty again!"

Otto's fate was repeated in 1886 – it struck Ludwig II. When the latter was taken away in Gudden's custody, he was in possession, as we have seen, of the latest details of Otto's case. Otto's confessor for many years, Abbot Haneberg from St. Boniface in Munich, was no doubt largely responsible for the fact that Otto never acted as Ludwig did in June 1886. On Whit Sunday, June 13th, Dr. Gudden would not allow the King to attend divine service.[38] This undoubtedly augmented Ludwig's despondency and desperation, as his deep roots in the Catholic faith were a great source of strength for him.

1866 – 1886 – 2001

During the years since the King's death much has changed on the European continent. But no matter how much has altered, particularly in Central Europe, people flock in their thousands to the Bayreuth Festival Theatre and to the musical drama whose creation by Richard Wagner was championed by Ludwig II – as well as to exhibitions featuring the King in Munich, London, Brussels and New York, and to the lonely King's castles; he failed to grasp the purpose and magnitude of the mission of Royal stewardship as conceived and practised by his father, Max II; but he fought a valiant battle against his inward affliction and for the idea of kingship.

Notes

1 Genealogical information on the Wittelsbachs can be found in Christian Haeutle, Genealogie des erlauchten Stammhauses Wittelsbach von dessen Wiedereinsetzung in das Herzogthum Bayern (11. Sept. 1180) bis herab auf unsere Tage, Munich 1870.

2 The serious, scholarly literature on King Ludwig II should not be confused with the semi-fictional works about him, particularly as the latter often mix facts with conjecture and fantasy in a completely arbitrary manner. There is neither an academically satisfactory biography of the King, nor a monograph on the history of his reign which can meet the demands of scholarship. – For the most comprehensive biographical information, cf. Gottfried von Böhm, Ludwig II König von Bayern, 2nd edition, Berlin 1924. – An informative description of the history of his reign is provided by Michael Doeberl, Entwicklungsgeschichte Bayerns III, ed. Max Spindler, Munich 1931, pp 362 ff. For the history of his reign up to 1871, cf. H. Rall, Bayerns politische Entwicklung 1848–1871, in: M. Spindler, Handbuch der bayerischen Geschichte IV/1, 1974, pp 225 ff., particularly pp 253 ff. The following article, on the period after 1871, contains factual and methodical errors. Cf. H. Rall, Archivalische Zeitschrift, vol. 72, 1976, p 175, review. Reliable literature is already available on individual problems concerning Ludwig's biography and the history of his reign. A selection is dealt with in the following notes.

3 Emil Roesle, Die Geisteskrankheit der bayerischen Könige Ludwig II. und Otto in der Sicht neuer genealogisch-erbbiologischer Methoden, in: Genealogisches Jahrbuch II, 1962, pp 101 ff.

4 Isabella Braun, Prinzessin Alexandra von Bayern, Eine biographische Skizze, 1875; Ludwig II, who possessed a copy of this biography, followed his father's example in supporting and encouraging her social work with sympathetic attention and understanding.

5 Heinrich von Srbik, Deutsche Einheit, Idee und Wirklichkeit von Villafranca bis Königrätz, IV, Munich 1942, pp 133 ff.

6 Eugen Franz, Ludwig Freiherr von der Pfordten, Munich 1938.

7 Hans Rall, Bayern und die Entscheidung des Jahres 1866, in: Bayerische Verwaltungsblätter VIII, 1966, pp 253–257.

8 Karl Hämmerle, Gustav von Schlör. Ein Beitrag zur bayerischen Geschichte des 19. Jahrhunderts, Leipzig/Erlangen 1926. I intend to produce a separate paper dealing with Ludwig II's handling of domestic affairs.

9 The most informative account of the relationship between the King and Richard Wagner is to be found in Otto Strobel, König Ludwig II. und Richard Wagner, Briefwechsel I–V, Karlsruhe 1936–39; the problematic nature of this relationship is covered by Sebastian Röckl, Ludwig II. und Richard Wagner, Munich 1913; Annette Kolb, König Ludwig II. von Bayern und Richard Wagner, Munich 1963. D. and M. Petzet, Die Richard-Wagner-Bühne König Ludwigs II. – München/Bayreuth, Munich 1970. Record: Musica Bavarica 803: Ballettmusik für Separatvorstellungen für König Ludwig II. von Bayern, ed. by Robert Münster. David E. R. George, Henrik Ibsen in Deutschland, Rezeption und Revision, Göttingen 1968, pp 18, 66 f. W. H. Eller, Ibsen in Germany 1870–1900, Boston 1918, refers to the Ibsen performance in Munich in 1875. This is not mentioned by Hans Wagner, 200 Jahre Münchner Theaterchronik 1750–1950, Munich 1960, but at the same time, he does not contradict Eller's statement. Wagner can naturally only provide a selective theatrical chronicle. Cf. also J. W. McFarlane, The Oxford Ibsen, vol. 2, Oxford 1960, pp 348, 370. Ibsen's "Doll's House" was given its first performance in 1880 in the Munich Residenztheater, (March 3rd, 1880); George, p 1925, H. Wagner, p 34. Ibsen himself, who had known Munich since 1875, moved there in 1880 and commented: "The air is so fresh, the people are so friendly, *the theatre is so good.* Here they let everyone live the way he wants", H. Wagner, p 34. K. Hommel, Die Separat-Vorstellungen vor König Ludwig II. von Bayern, Munich 1963.

10 Erika Wilk, König Ludwig II. und das Schauspiel, dissertation, Munich 1980.

11 Böhm, loc. cit., p 70.

12 Eugen Franz, König Ludwig II. von Bayern, das königliche Kabinett, das Ministerium und das Bayerische Volk 1864–66, in: Staat und Volkstum. Neue Studien zur bairischen und deutschen Geschichte und Volkskunde, commemorative publication in honour of Karl Al. von Müller, Diessen near Munich 1933, pp 82–98.

13 Hans Rall, Ausblicke auf Weltentwicklung und Religion im Kreise Max' II. und Ludwigs II., in: Land und Volk, Herrschaft und Staat in der Geschichte und Geschichtsforschung Bayerns (Zeitschrift für bayer. Landesgeschichte, vol. 27), Munich 1964, pp 488–522, esp. 503 ff.

14 Concerning the problems and sources dealt with here, cf. Hans Rall, Das Altarsakrament im Schicksal König Ludwigs II. von Bayern, in: Festgabe des Vereins für Diözesangeschichte von München und Freising zum Münchener Eucharistischen Weltkongress, ed. by A. W. Ziegler, 1960, pp 160–179, esp. 166.

15 Detlev Vogel, Der Stellenwert des Militärischen in Bayern 1849–1875, 1980.

16 No political biography of Hohenlohe exists. Information on his work as a Bavarian minister from 1867 to 1870 and also on his later connections with Bavaria is to be found in: Friedrich Curtis (Ed.), Denkwürdigkeiten des Fürsten Chlodwig zu Hohenlohe und Schillingsfürst I–II, Stuttgart/Leipzig 1907, and Karl Alexander von Müller, Fürst Chlodwig zu Hohenlohe-Schillingsfürst, Denkwürdigkeiten der Reichskanzlerzeit, Stuttgart/Berlin 1931.

17 Böhm, loc. cit., p 391. R. Sexau, Fürst und Arzt (see note 34 below), pp 173 ff.

18 H. Rall, England und Bayern im Frühjahr 1870, in: O. Kuhn, Großbritannien und Deutschland, commemorative publication for J. W. P. Bourke, pp 247 ff.

19 Cf. Günther Müller, König Max II. von Bayern und die soziale Frage, dissertation, Munich 1964.

20 Elmar Roeder, Die politischen Kämpfe des "Volksboten" Zanders und die Anfänge der bayer. Patriotenpartei, typewritten dissertation, Munich 1971. Helmut Kistler, Der bayerische Landtag 1871/72, typewritten dissertation, Munich 1957, esp. pp 5 ff. Cf. also Theodor Schieder, Die Kleindeutsche Partei in Bayern in den Kämpfen um die nationale Einheit 1863–71, Munich 1936.

21 Michael Doeberl, Bayern und die Bismarckische Reichsgründung, Munich/Berlin 1925, p 92.

22 Hans Rall, Bismarcks Reichsgründung und die Geldwünsche aus Bayern, in: Zeitschrift für bayerische Landesgeschichte 1959, pp 396–497. – The territorial aspirations concerned the Wittelsbach Palatinate right of the Rhine, or alternatively a corridor between the Palatinate and Bavarian Lower Franconia.

23 The subsidies for Richard Wagner and the costs of the castle building were provided for by the Cabinet fund, as is evidenced by the books of the Cabinet fund in the Privy Household Archives in Munich. On the subsidies for Wagner, cf. also Otto Strobel, Neue Wagner-Forschungen, Veröffentlichungen der Richard-Wagner-Forschungsstätte Bayreuth, Karlsruhe 1943, esp. pp 101 ff. and Rall-Petzet, p 11.

24 Emperor Napoleon III had the King shown the palace in July, 1864.

25 Heinrich Kreisel, Die Schlösser Ludwigs II. von Bayern, Darmstadt 1955, p 26. H. G. Evers, see Note 30 below. Cf. also Louise von Kobell, König Ludwig II. von Bayern und die Kunst, Munich 1898.

26 H. Goldschmidt, H. Kaiser, H. Thimme, Ein Jahrhundert Deutscher Geschichte, 1928, vol. 46. – H. Rall, König Ludwig II. und Bismarcks Ringen um Bayern 1870/71, unter Auswertung unbekannter englischer, preussischer und bayerischer Quellen dargestellt, Munich 1973.

27 Baron Fritz von Rummel, Das Ministerium Lutz und seine Gegner 1871–82, Munich 1935. – In the paper mentioned in Note 7, I intend to deal in more detail with the relationship between the King and Baron G. A. v. Franckenstein. In 1875, as in 1872, Ludwig considers taking up residence on the Canary Islands in his despair.

28 Rummel, loc. cit., pp 57, 173 f.

29 Ludwig II's letters to Bismarck should not be looked on as mere confessions. The King was by no means "politically as immature as a child", as Doeberl, loc. cit., p 165, mistakenly assumed. He wrote the letters out of political considerations, as we can today recognize from a confidential remark. Bismarck entered into correspondence with King Ludwig II and also with his successor, Prince Regent Luitpold, in the political interests of his Imperial policy, and it is significant that he later published a selection of his correspondence with Ludwig in his memoirs, "Gedanken und Erinnerungen". Cf. in this connection also Karl Alexander von Müller, Unbekannte Briefe Bismarcks an Ludwig II., in: Süddeutsche Monatshefte Juni 1932, pp 632 ff., esp. p 634 Note 1. For information on this complex of problems, cf. Irmgard v. Barton, known as v. Stedman, Die preussische Gesandtschaft in München als Instrument der Reichspolitik in Bayern von den Anfängen der Reichsgründung bis zu Bismarcks Entlassung, dissertation, Munich 1967, in: Miscellanea Bavarica Monacensia, ed. by K. Bosl and M. Schattenhofer, vol. 2, 1967.

30 Cf. the essay mentioned in Note 13, esp. pp 517 ff. H. G. Evers, Tod, Macht und Raum als Bereiche der Architektur, 1939 (chapter "Herrenchiemsee" pp 199–282), reprinted 1971. Evers is at present working on a substantial monograph on King Ludwig II and the buildings he commissioned.

31 Cf. Note 14.

32 Cf. Rupert Hacker, Ludwig II. von Bayern in Augenzeugenberichten, Düsseldorf 1966, pp 282 ff. He had the permission of HRH Duke Albrecht of Bavaria to use material from the Privy Household Archives.

33 Cf. Ludwig Schrott, Der Prinzregent, ein Lebensbild aus Stimmen seiner Zeit, Munich 1962. – Ludwig II's letters to Luitpold demonstrate that in 1870/71 their cooperation was founded on trust: cf. Rall, König Ludwig II. und Bismarcks Ringen um Bayern 1870/1871, 1973, pp 143 ff., 161 ff.

34 Gottfried von Böhm's detailed information (cf. Note 2) was later added to by various sources, e.g. Karl Alexander von Müller, Dokumente zur Geschichte der Entmündigung Ludwigs II., in: Süddeutsche Monatshefte Juli 1930, pp 679 ff.; Fridolin Solleder, König Ludwigs II. letzte Tage auf Neuschwanstein, in: Das Bayerland 1926, pp 33 ff.; Franz Müller, Die letzten Tage König Ludwigs II., in: Süddeutsche Monatshefte 1929; various reports are analysed, though without particulars, by Richard Sexau, Die Tragödie König Ludwigs II., Fluchtversuch nicht Selbstmord, in: Der Zwiebelturm 1957, vol. 12, 1958, vol. 1; Richard Sexau, Fürst und Arzt, Dr. med. Herzog Carl Theodor in Bayern, Graz 1963, pp 305 ff., 322 ff (with references).

35 Böhm, loc. cit., p 689.

36 The psychological and historical impression which the figure of Ludwig II made on his contemporaries and later generations is illustrated by Anton Sailer, Bayerns Märchenkönig, Munich 1961. This is not the place to consider the more fantastic psychological essays from the pens of German, French and Anglo-Saxon authors.

37 Ludwig Schrott, Herrscher Bayerns, 1974, p 216.

38 Böhm (Note 2), p 692; the Privy Councillor Ludwig Klug had recorded in a note dated June 26th, 1886 in Munich: "On June 12th of this year, I enquired of His Majesty asked whether Divine Service should be held in the private church at Schloss Berg, on Sunday, June 13th, as was customary when His Majesty was in residence, whereupon His Majesty sent me instructions (via whom?) only to order Divine Service for Sunday, June 20th." Crailsheim added an undated note to this memorandum: "Confidential note: Councillor Klug has in his possession no documents concerning this matter. I therefore felt it necessary to require him to make the above statement."

Michael Petzet

The Life of King Ludwig II
in Pictures

Hereditary Prince Ludwig in his first year, 1846. Coloured photograph after an original by Adolf Grotefend, signed below right "A. Grotefend". 8" x 6". – WAF, Inv. no. 41

Hereditary Prince Ludwig with a picture-book. Water-colour by Ernst Rietschel, 1847, signed below left "E. Rietschel". 10" x 8". – WAF, Inv. no. 44

Crown Prince Ludwig with a drum and box of bricks. Coloured photograph after a
water-colour by Ernst Rietschel, signed below left "E. Rietschel 1850"; below right, Queen Marie,
Ludwig II's mother, has written "Christmas 1850 (from the King)". 13" x 10". –
WAF Inv. no. 46

Queen Marie with her sons, Crown Prince Ludwig and Prince Otto, while feeding the swans.
Coloured photograph after a water-colour by Ernst Rietschel, 1850. 16" x 12". – WAF, Inv. no. 47

70

King Maximilian II with Queen Marie and his sons Ludwig and Otto at Hohenschwangau. Lithograph
c. 1850, signed below "Composed and drawn from life by E. CORRENS – Drawn on stone by
J. WOELFFLE". 34" x 24". – BSV, Inv. no. 37

Crown Prince Ludwig and Prince Otto in huntsman's costume on a rocky slope, left Otto, right Ludwig.
Photograph by Joseph Albert, 1857. – BSV, Inv. no. 53

The Royal Family out walking at Hohenschwangau. Photograph by Joseph Albert, 1859. From right to left:
unidentified gentleman-in-waiting, King Maximilian II, Countess Fugger, Prince Otto,
Crown Prince Ludwig, Queen Marie. – BSV, Inv. no. 3245

Ludwig II in the uniform of a Bavarian general with the cross of the Hubertus-Knights-Order.
Portrait by Wilhelm Tauber, signed "W. Tauber 1864". Oil on canvas, 30" x 22". – BSV, Inv. no. 10

Ludwig II disembarking at Schloss Berg, in the foreground the King with a rose in his left hand, right two footmen holding horses, in the background Schloss Berg, left three sailors in front of the paddle steamer "Tristan". Water-colour by Erich Correns, signed below left "Er. Correns./fec. 1867." 13" x 19". – WAF, Inv. no. 102

Page 75 top:
Ludwig II greeting Emperor Francis Joseph and Empress Elisabeth of Austria in front of the spa at Bad Kissingen, June 18th, 1864; left of the King, the Empress of Russia. Water-colour by Johannes Maar, signed below right "Joh. Maar/1864". 9" x 12". – WAF, Inv. no. B VIII 6

Page 75 bottom:
Ludwig II taking a morning walk with his aide-de-camp in the gardens of Schloss Berg. Water-colour by Ludwig Quaglio, signed below left "L. Quaglio. fec. 1865". 10" x 14". – WAF, Inv. no. B VIII 7

Page 76:
Crown Prince Ludwig. Photograph by Joseph Albert, May 14th, 1861. – BSV, Inv. no. 71

Page 77:
Crown Prince Ludwig in the uniform of the Royal Infantry Regiment. Photograph by Joseph Albert, 1863. – BSV, Inv. no. 68

76

Crown Prince Ludwig. Photograph by Joseph Albert, 1863. – BSV, Inv. no. 69

Ludwig II in General's uniform with coronation robe. Portrait by Ferdinand Piloty, 1865, signed below right "Ferd. Piloty", top left, below the Bavarian Royal Coat of Arms, the inscription: "LUDOVICUS II. / BAVARIAE REX / MDCCCLXV." Oil on canvas, 134" x 65". – BSV, Inv. no. 901

Portrait of Richard Wagner, gift from the composer to the King, presumably 1864, signed in Wagner's hand:
"You alone give me strength to thank You, through Your unshaking Royal trust. Richard Wagner."
Water-coloured photograph, oval, 34" high. – BSV, Inv. no. 609

Page 81 top:
Model of the proposed Munich festival theatre to be erected approximately on the site of the present
Friedensengel, for Richard Wagner's musical dramas, according to plans by Gottfried Semper, 1865–66.
Reconstruction by Hermann R. Dürr, 1927 (the original model was destroyed in the last war). Length 88",
width 87", height 20" (without bridge). – BSV, Inv. no. 606

Final scene in the Munich premiere of the "Fliegender Holländer", December 4th, 1864. Water-colour by Michael Echter, signed below left "M. Echter/15/4 1874". 19" x 25". – BSV, Inv. no. 697

Final scene in the Munich premiere of "Tristan und Isolde", June 10th, 1865. Grey-washed pencil drawing by M. Echter, 1867. 19" x 26". – BSV, Inv. no. 632

Final scene in the Munich première of the "Meistersinger von Nürnberg", June 21st, 1868. Water colour by M. Echter, signed below right "M. Echter./1872". 20" x 26". – BSV, Inv. no. 712

Tsarina Maria Alexandrovna visiting Schloss Berg, 26th September, 1868; in the foreground the King with the Tsarina after leaving the paddle steamer "Tristan", in the background an illumination with the Russian Imperial Crown and Imperial Flag. Watercolour by Josef Watter, signed below right "J. Watter München". 14" x 21". – BSV, Inv. no. 100

Baron Ludwig von der Tann, General and Bavarian Chief of Staff, 1866. Photograph by Franz Hanfstaengl. –
BSV, Inv. no. 107

Ludwig II on horseback, painting by Fedor Dietz, 1866. Oil on canvas, 84" x 70". –
Marstallmuseum Schloss Nymphenburg. – BSV, Inv. no. W 78

The later Empress Elisabeth of Austria on horseback, 1853; in the background Schloss Possenhofen. Engraving after a painting by Piloty and Adam entitled "Empress Elisabeth of Austria as a Princess before Her marriage at Possenhofen, MDCCCLIII ...", signed below "Portrait painted from life by Carl Piloty – engraved by A. Fleischmann – horse painted from nature by Franz Adam". 35" x 27". – BSV, Inv. no. 159

Duchess Sophie Charlotte, daughter of Duke Max of Bavaria. Photograph by Franz Hanfstaengl, 1867 (?). –
BSV, Inv. no. 91

Betrothed: Ludwig II and Sophie Charlotte, Photograph by Joseph Albert, 1867. – BSV, Inv. no. 90

Ludwig II in the regalia of a Knight of St. George. Photograph by Joseph Albert, 1866. – BSV, Inv. no. 96

Chapter meeting of the Bavarian household order of St. George in the inner audience chamber of the Rich Rooms at the Munich Residenz, April 24th, 1869; under the throne baldachin Ludwig II as Grand Master of the Order. Water-colour by Friedrich Eibner and Julius Frank, 1869, signed below right "Jul. Frank / u. / F. Eibner". 18" x 23". – WAF

Page 91 top:
Ludwig II conferring his first accolade at the anniversary of the Bavarian household order of St. George in the chapel of the Residenz, Munich, April 24th, 1867. Water-colour by Franz Seitz. 17" x 34". – WAF

Page 91 bottom:
Ludwig II at the festival banquet of the Bavarian household order of St. George in the St. George's Room of the Munich Residenz, April 29th, 1868. Water-colour by Friedrich Eibner and Julius Frank, signed below right "Jul. Frank / u. / F. Eibner / 1869". 18" x 24". – WAF

91

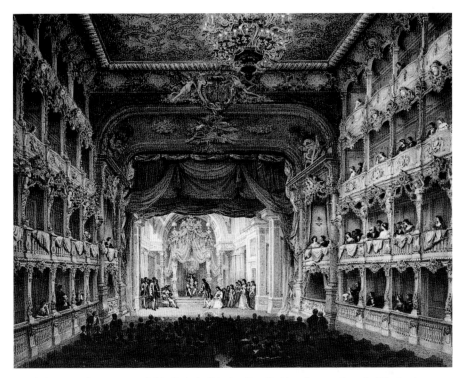

A theatre performance attended by Ludwig II in the Altes Residenztheater, where the King's private performances were held from 1864 on. Water-colour by Gustav Seeberger, signed below left "G. Seeberger./1867". 17" x 23". – WAF

Page 93 top:
Ludwig II's winter garden on the roof of the north tract (Festsaalbau) of the Munich Residenz, built by Carl von Effner, 1868, and demolished after the King's death. Photograph by Joseph Albert. – BSV, Inv. no. 554

Page 93 bottom:
Festival banquet given by Ludwig II in the ballroom of the north tract of the Munich Residenz on the occasion of the marriage of Archduchess Gisela, the daughter of Emperor Francis Joseph, and Prince Leopold Maximilian Joseph, the son of the future Prince Regent Luitpold. 1873. Water-colour, signed below left "F (= Friedrich) Eibner u. Wiedemann 1873". 22" x 29". – WAF

Count Otto von Bray-Steinburg, Chief Minister, Minister of Crown Affairs and Foreign Minister, 1870–71.
Photograph by Franz Hanfstaengl, c. 1870. – BSV, Inv. no. 1006

The Feldherrnhalle, with a bust of Ludwig II, decorated for the victory march into Munich, July 16th, 1871.
Photograph by Joseph Albert (?), 1871. – BSV, Inv. no. 111

Page 96:
Crown Prince Frederick William of Prussia in General's uniform. Photograph by Franz Hanfstaengl, c. 1870. –
BSV, Inv. no. 1003

96

Bavarian troops returning to Munich under the command of Prince Frederick William, Crown Prince of Prussia and the German Empire, march past King Ludwig II, 16th June, 1871. Watercolour by Alois Bach, signed below right "Bach fec.". 12" x 20". – BSV, Inv. no. 113

Page 98:
Prince Otto of Bavaria. Ludwig II's brother, as Major-General and commander of the 5th Light Horse. Photograph by Joseph Albert, c. 1870. – BSV, Inv. no. 224

98

View of Linderhof, which was built by Ludwig II as from 1869, from the upper garden pavilion across the cascade and towards the palace and the south terraces. Water-colour by Heinrich Breling, 1882, signed below right "H. Breling". 10" x 9". – WAF, Inv. no. 275

Page 100 top:
The Linderhof building site, 1874/75 with the ground floor of the palace, the pool, and the south terraces taking shape. Photograph from 1874/75. – BSV, Inv. no. 272

Page 100 bottom:
Ludwig II being rowed round the grotto of Venus, Linderhof. Illustration after a drawing by Robert Assmus in the "Gartenlaube", 1886, pp 648/49

Linderhof in the park designed by Hofgartendirektor Carl von Effner. View over the Terrace Garden on the Main Parterre in front of the building, the cascade in the background

The grotto of Venus in red illumination, built for Ludwig II in 1876/77 taking the decoration of Richard Wagner's "Tannhäuser" (1st act) as a model. Water-colour by Heinrich Breling 1881, signed below right "H. Breling". 9" x 13". – WAF, Inv. Nr. 296

Ludwig II. Photograph by Joseph Albert 1875. – BSV, Inv. no. 118

"Hunding's Hut" near Linderhof, built by Ludwig II, 1876, modelled on the sets for the first act of
Richard Wagner's "Walküre". Water-colour by Heinrich Breling, 1882, signed below right "H. Breling".
13" x 22". – WAF, Inv. no. 300

Linderhof palace in winter, with Ludwig II's state sleigh drawn by six horses. Water-colour by
Heinrich Breling, 1880/81, signed below "H. Breling". 16" x 24". – BSV, Inv. no. 126

Ludwig II on a night sleigh trip from Neuschwanstein castle to Linderhof; the state sleigh, which is now
on display in the Marstallmuseum at Nymphenburg, was built by Syrius Eberle and Lorenz Gedon after
a design by Franz Seitz. Painting by R. Wening, c. 1880. Oil on canvas, 32" x 50". –
Marstallmuseum Schloss Nymphenburg, Inv. no. G 1186

Page 105:

Ludwig II as Grand Master of the Bavarian household order of St. George, holding the "Sword of
St. Christopher" (Treasury of the Munich Residenz). Painting by Gabriel Schachinger, only completed after
the King's death, signed below left "Gab. Schachinger München 1987". Oil on canvas, 103" x 69". –
BSV, Inv. no. L. II.-Mus. 3186 (or 6 respecitvely; formerly BStGS Inv. 7814)

The King's bedroom at Linderhof, extended in 1884 after a design by Eugen Drollinger. Embroidery: only the Bavarian coat of arms by Dora and Mathilde Jörres was executed until the King's death. Ceiling (Apoll's Chariot) by Ludwig Lesker

Page 107:

Linderhof, west facade with statue of Apoll by Franz Walker in the central niche; in the foreground the western parterre with statue of Fama, gilded zinc casting by Walker. The stone facade was erected after plans by Georg von Dollmann (1873/74) around a plain wooden construction of the rooms of the "Royal Villa" (in parts built since 1870)

Herrenchiemsee palace, garden facade of the "new Versailles" (planned by Georg von Dollmann for Linderhof in the first place) for which the foundation stone was laid on Herrenwörth island in Lake Chiemsee on May 21ˢᵗ, 1878. In the foreground the southern basin of the Main Parterre with the Fama group by the sculptor Wilhelm von Ruemann

Page 108:
Herrenchiemsee palace, Hall of Mirrors, modelled on Versailles and true to its scale, but with the spectacular design that is not preserved at Versailles

The uncompleted west gardens, Herrenchiemsee, view from the ground floor, over the Apollo pool and the canal, towards the lake. Unsigned water-colour (attributed to Heinrich Breling), c. 1880. 9" x 14". – BSV, Inv. no. 380

Herrenchiemsee palace, design for the west front by Georg Dollmann, 1875 (the foundation stone of the palace was laid in 1878). Water-coloured line drawing. 13" x 49". – BSV, Inv. no. 329

Neuschwanstein castle, layout (foundation stone was laid in 1869) by stage designer Christian Jank, signed below right "Chr. Jank 69". Gouache, 24" x 30". – WAF, Inv. no. 402

Page 112:
Neuschwanstein, "Sängersaal", hall modelled on the Wartburg by Julius Hofmann, painted in 1883/84 by August Spiefl with scenes from Wolfram von Eschenbach's "Parzifal"

Neuschwanstein, seen from the East, in its singular location above Lake Alpsee

Ludwig II and the actor Josef Kainz during their Swiss tour, June 1881. Photograph by Syneberg, Lucerne. –
Theatermuseum Munich

Page 114 top:
Ludwig II driving from Linderhof through Ettal. Water-colour by Otto von Ruppert, signed below right
"O. v. Ruppert 1881". 9" x 11". – WAF, Inv. no. L. II.-Mus. 124

Page 114 bottom:
"Diotwina", Ludwig's horse, in front of the king's house on Grammersberg. Painting by Friedrich Wilhelm
Pfeiffer (1868). Picture taken after restoration in 1988 – Nymphenburg, Marstallmuseum. –
WAF, Inv. no. W 51

Count Dürckheim, ADC to Ludwig II, 1886. Photograph by Joseph Albert, c. 1880. – BSV, Inv. no. 140

Ludwig II, photograph by Joseph Albert, 1886. – Privy Household Archives

Schloss Berg beside the Starnberger See. Water-colour by Max Kuhn, signed below right "M. Kuhn 1875".
8" x 11". – WAF, Inv. no. B VIII 26

Ludwig II lying in state, June 16th–17th, 1886, the dead King in the regalia of a Knight of St. Hubert.
Photograph by J. Albert. – BSV, Inv. no. 151

119

Ludwig II's funeral procession, June 19th, 1886, passing the former cadets' college (Karlsplatz), right the gate to the Old Botanical Gardens with the Crystal Palace in the background.
Photograph by Franz Hanfstaengl, 1886. – BSV, Inv. no. 147

Ludwig II's funeral procession, June 19th, 1886; the cortège arriving at St. Michael's Church.
Photograph from 1886. – BSV, Inv. no. 145

King Ludwig's sarcophagus in the crypt of St. Michael, Munich. – WAF

121

Berg on Starnberger See, Votive Chapel, built in remembrance of King Ludwig's death. – WAF

Statue of Ludwig II as Grand Master of the Bavarian household order of St. George, statue after a clay model by Elisabeth Ney, executed in marble by Friedrich Ochs, signed on the base "Elisabeth Ney fee. 1870 – Fr. Ochs fec. Marmors". White marble. Height 6' 8". – Inv. no. 1

123

Michael Petzet

King Ludwig II
and the Fine Arts

News of the King's death in 1886 sent shock waves throughout Europe and moved Paul Verlaine to write a sonnet honouring him as "the only true King of the century", though, Ludwig II himself refused to be a "people's King". In retrospect, Ludwig II appears as the embodiment of the last glorious epoch of Bavarian history, one of the most outstanding builders among a long succession of ancestors belonging to the Wittelsbacher dynasty. At the same time, he was a most eminent patron of the theater whose building projects are now indisputably viewed as significant, not only in terms of art history and Historicism, but also procure special interest due to their continuous interrelationships with the world of theater: from Neuschwanstein to the operas of Richard Wagner, from Linderhof, Herrenchiemsee and the "oriental" buildings, to Munich's famous "private performances".[1] It is here in the Singers' Hall of Neuschwanstein, the Mirror Gallery of Herrenchiemsee, or the grotto of Venus at Linderhof that one can best perceive and grasp the "lonely King". His essence permeates these and all the other tabernacles of art which were built according to his ideas or only planned "historically". The King incorporated a triple role, so to speak, as director, spectator and leading performer in the private drama of his own making. Retreating more and more from the world after the political and personal disappointments in the early years of his reign, the King became an autocratic theater director who demanded that new dramas associated with certain historical personalities and events be staged again and again. As a spectator he was never really satisfied but always longing to be able to experience new theater productions. In his role as leading performer he could strut upon the stage in a multitude of costumes: Ludwig as Lohengrin, Siegfried, Parsifal, Ludwig as Louis XIV or Louis XV, Ludwig as Oberon.

The different roles of the King, however, were played out in quite different worlds. The works of the composer Richard Wagner, for example, belonged to the "medieval" world which the swan, Ludwig II's favorite animal, held sway over. The staging of "model performances" of a number of the composer's operas, such as the memorable Munich première of "Tristan" (1865) and the "Meistersinger" (1868), as well as the first complete cycle of the "Ring" (1876) and "Parsifal" (1882) at the Festival Hall in Bayreuth, was first made possible by the King.[2] In the following, however, the focus will not be on the King as the great Maecenas of Wagner's work, who the composer quite rightly honoured as "cocreator", but rather on Ludwig II's role as an unusually imaginative builder who restlessly worked at creating the different "theatrical settings" of his life. After the initially predominating "medieval" world, there soon followed, under the sign of the lily and the sun – the symbol of the Sun King – the world of the Bourbons and then the "oriental" world.

Heinrich Kreisel was the first scholar to recognize the importance of the royal palaces for the cultural and art history of the nineteenth century and to study Ludwig II's building projects under the aspect of the different spheres of interest which dominated the King's view of the world. These three spheres can be paraphrased under the headings of the Holy Grail, the Sun and the Moon:[3] the "medieval" castles under the sign of the Holy Grail (Neuschwanstein and Falkenstein), buildings in the later baroque and rococo style under the sign of the sun (the King's apartments in his Munich residence, Linderhof with its Hubertus Pavillon and theatre project, Herrenchiemsee), buildings in oriental style under the sign of the moon (Schachen, the Moorish kiosk and Moroccan house at Linderhof). The King himself makes references to two of these signs in his diary: "Under the sign of the sun (Nec pluribus impar) and the moon (The Orient! Reincarnation with Oberon's magic horn) ...".[4]

Before ever becoming acquainted with Wagner, the King had been exposed to the medieval world in the shape and spirit of Hohenschwangau. Originally the ancestral seat of the lords of Schwangau, the castle had been purchased by the King's father Maximilian II and in accordance with plans by the stage designer Domenico Quaglio "restored to its original medieval form"[5], as the crown prince Ludwig phrases it in one of his childhood sketches. At the age of twelve he read "auf dem Spiegel des Alpsees" (On the Mirror of Mountain Lake) and "Ring des Nibelungen" (The Ring of the Nibelungs) at the foot of the castle. Long before his fateful encounter with Wagner's "Lohengrin", the wall paintings in his father's castle had familiarized him with the saga. Later he moved from the crown prince's quarters into his father's apartment in the castle where the royal bedchamber was decorated with paintings of characters from Rinaldo and Armida. He transformed the chamber into a little "spatial work of art" by adding in 1864/65 some further features, since lost. These additaments already evidence the characteristic peculiarities of his later art projects which always demonstrated a close affinity to the stage. On the ceiling, painted as the night sky, the theater mechanic Penkmayr attached "an illumination for the night in the shape of the moon" which was later augmented by stars and a rainbow machine as well as a "stone fountain" and three artificial orange trees.[6] Soon feeling irritated by his mother's "prose" in Hohenschwangau – "this paradise on earth I have populated with my ideals thus making me happy"[7] – he began plans for building a castle in 1868 "in the authentic style of the German knight's castle of old"[8] on the site of the ruins of Vorderhohenschwangau. The typical late romantic idea of "reconstruction", later reappearing in plans for Falkenstein in 1883, was linked to the idea of a new swan knight's castle. The swan was also Maximilian's favorite animal and as a heraldic symbol the motive is reproduced in many different forms, from paintings to the applied arts, in his old castle which paved the way for Ludwig's art in many respects.

The name "Neuschwanstein" for "Neue Burg Hohenschwangau" (New Castle Hohenschwangau) was only used after 1886, the year of the King's death when, along with his other castles, it was opened to the public for sightseeing on August 1st, 1886. In accordance with Ludwig's wishes the project's style changed from one of a small "robber-knight's castle" to that of a monumental "Romanesque" castle. Oriented on Nuremberger models with late gothic details, the castle with its five-storied hall keep is reminiscent of the hall keep at Wartburg which the King visited in 1867 in preparation for a new staging of "Tannhäuser". Viewed today, curiously enough, as the quintessence of a "medieval castle", Neuschwanstein is nonetheless not a copy of any specific medieval building but rather a unique creation of Historicism. Very revealing is the reason given for rejecting the suggestion of a painter who wanted, in the spirit of late romanticism, to put the castle together out of pieces copied from different, medieval buildings: "By the wish of His Majesty the King the new castle is to be built in the Romanesque style. Since we are now, though, writing the year 1871 and have advanced centuries beyond the time in which the Romanesque style came into being, there can be do doubt that the progress that has been made in the fields of art and science since then should also be applied to our advantage in the building venture at hand ... I would also not like to support the idea that we should return completely to the past and ignore experiences that, if they had been known of at the time, certainly would have been implemented."[9]

The extent to which the King also paid attention to the correct "style" in connection with interior decoration is illustrated by his criticism of a drawing by Julius Hofmann for the bed canopy of a bedchamber: "The design details are not precise enough, His Majesty envisions the wood carvings as much more delicate, with more filigree. The canopy itself should be highest at the center with decorations gracing the back, front and both sides!"[10] The bedroom and adjoining chapel based on a design by Peter Herwegen are the only showcases for furniture in the "late gothic" style. Their comparatively "historical" forms can clearly be distinguished from the "not wholly in the spirit of the style permeated" Biedermeier neo-gothic style of Hohenschwangau. The rest of the furnishings with the re-occurring theme of the swan were designed in "Romanesque" style. Julius Hofmann worked with his father as a young man for the Archduke Maximilian at Castle Miramare near Trieste and in 1864 was contracted to transform the town hall of Mexico into a residence for the future emperor. At Neuschwanstein he proved to be a virtuoso, a highly skilled designer, master of every "style". He was joined by a team of history painters for the wall painting program developed in part by Ludwig himself in cooperation with the scholar Dr. Hyazinth Holland, a specialist for medieval iconography.[11] In keeping with a castle which was supposed to one day become a "temple" to Wagner – though the composer himself never stepped foot in it – practically only motifs touching on themes from Wagnerian operas were planned. In accordance with a command by the King in 1879, however, the pictures had to be made to correspond to "the specifications of the saga and not to those of Wagner's works".[12] In complete contrast to his grandfather, Ludwig in his lifetime purchased only a single notable painting, Feuerbach's "Medea". He was not interested in any original artists of note but "only in painters who have carefully studied medieval poetry".[13] In other words, he wanted history painters who would adhere exactly to the King's artistic conception based on his literary studies and whose guiding principle was the poetic "transfiguration" of authentic or supposed "historical truths". While during the same period an artist such as Wilhelm Leibl was painting in Bavaria, the King only cared about the "what" and less about the "how". Though his specifications and criticisms seemed to only deal with matters of form, they were also always an attempt to evoke a certain style. Since he wanted to see exactly what was being illustrated, he rejected any "imprecise" manner of depiction and characterized pictures painted in a flighty style as "sloppy" while condemning any exaggerations as "caricatures". Naturally, there was also no room for anything "commonplace" in these history paintings. In consciousness of his own dignity, the King demanded at the same time an "exalted" and "natural" manner of depiction. Finally, one of Ludwig's most difficult demands was his insistence on setting tight deadlines in complete disregard of "the well-known indolence of artists".[14] The deadline for completing the living quarters of Neuschwanstein is an example: it took the combined, desperate efforts of the painters Hauschild, Spiefl, Piloty, Aigner and Ille, working day and night, to finish the rooms by the first day of the Christmas holidays 1881.

The basically second-rate works of this team of painters accrue special value when viewed within the framework of Neuschwanstein as a collective work of art. From 1868 on the first basic design sketches were not developed by a history painter but rather by the stage painter Christian Junk.[15] Part of the basic concept included distinct stage design ideas which an army of painters and artisans were charged with implementing, first under the direction of the architect Eduard Riedel and then his successors Georg Dollmann (from 1874 on) and Julius Hofmann (from 1884 on).[16] Immersed in his own conceits of stage design and particularly interested in the staging of Wagner's operas, Ludwig even came into conflict with the "Maestro" himself in connection with a new staging of "Lohengrin".[17] Years before building began on the castle Ludwig, who later on occasion loved to dress up as Lohengrin, had already implemented a staging of the first act, "On the Bank of the Schelde", depicting the arrival of the Swan Knight at the Alpine lake at the foot of the castle. Christian Jank modeled his plans for the castle courtyard on the stage décor from the second act of "Lohengrin", "The Castle Courtyard of Antwerp". They were obviously based on Angelo II Quaglio's castle courtyard designs for the 1867 staging of "Lohengrin" in Munich. Finally, there are also the blueprints for the bedchamber of the ladies' bower at Neuschwanstein inspired by the bridal suite from the third act.

The new castle as envisioned by its builder, however, was to be not only Lohengrin's castle but also, at the same time, Tannhäuser's castle: In the same manner as Heinrich Döll, the landscape specialist among Munich's stage designers, recreated a historically authentic picture of the Wartburg against the background of the Wartburg valley with a system of set-scenes, the King wanted his castle to appear to rise from rugged cliffs above the Pöllat ravine against the background of the breathtaking Bavarian mountains. Plans for a Minstrel's Hall to be modelled on the Festival Hall of Wartburg – itself not completed till 1867 – were also part of the project right from the beginning. The plan of the Wartburg hall, at the express orders of King Friedrich Wilhelm IV issued in 1858, had acted as a model for the stage design in the second act of the "Tannhäuser" première in Berlin.

When Wagner prescribed the Paris plans based on his own specifications for a new staging of the opera in Munich in 1867, the Privy Councillor Düfflipp reported the King's objections: "Here the Wartburg Hall is all in the gothic style which His Majesty regards as an unjustifiable anachronism because at the time the Tannhäuser sagas took place the byzantine building style would have been well-known but not the gothic style".[18] Since Wagner insisted on keeping the Paris Festival Hall design based on the English gothic style, the King, as concerns this stage design, was forced to give in. However, he had Christian Jank combine elements from both the Festival Hall as well as the Minstrel's Arcade of the Minstrel's Hall at Wartburg to create the new Minstrel's Hall at Neuschwanstein. It, in turn, served as a model for later stage design sets of "Tannhäuser".

Thus Neuschwanstein integrates stage designs from both "Lohengrin" and "Tannhäuser". The original plans call for the construction of a large bathchamber formed out of rock where the small grotto room leading off from the study was later built. Interestingly, Ludwig's father Maximilian had had a highly original bathchamber of red marble stone in the form of a cave built on the ground floor of the Lion's Tower at Hohenschwangau. Due to the lack of a suitable place, the idea for the large-scale grotto were then superimposed on that for a grotto planned by the Director of the Royal Gardens Effner in the park of Linderhof palace. This was made official in a decree on December 15th, 1875 and the work completed by the "landscape sculptor" August Dirigl by 1877.[19] Ludwig wanted to connect the grotto of Hörsel Mountain from "Tannhäuser" here with the "Blue Grotto". At the same time he also had it staged in the private performances. The King's enthusiasm for the Blue Grotto is typical of the times, the general popularity of grottos finding its expression at that period in exhibitions as well as in the construction of large-scale aquariums. The Master of the Horse Horning was even sent to Capri on two separate occasions in order to allow the "blueness" of the grotto sink into his consciousness. The grotto is a highly characteristic creation of the 19th century, which visualizes various aspects of not just Ludwig II's art. Its distinct tendency to combine stage design components, natural elements, and architecture can be seen in many exhibitions and conservatories (such as Ludwig's Munich winter garden). This "total" theatre, the ultimate peepshow stage, gave the lonely visitor the complete illusion of a stage simultaneously functioning as an auditorium. In contrast to the private performances in which the dark background of the auditorium divided attender and stage, the spectator – sitting on or at the edge of the stage in a skiff moving across the water or in one of the various "box seats" – experiences the "action" which only consists here in the changing colours and, by changing one's standpoint, changing views. The grotto of Hörsel Mountain, floodlit in red with the picture of the Venus Mountain scene painted by August Heckel, could be transformed into the Blue Grotto with a waterfall. It was possible to even catch a vista of the open countryside or the nearby castle against the framework of the grotto.

Hidden behind the illusion of massive rock held together by a skeleton of iron, were the most modern technical devices: a complicated system of plumbing to supply the lake and waterfall with water, a wave-making maschine, a warm air heating system that had to keep the temperature at a constant of 16° Réaumur and one of the first electrical power plants in Bavaria with a number of the recently discovered dynamos which powered the arc-lamps as well as the rainbow maschine. The King, who at one point is supposed to have said: "I don't want to know how it's done, I just want to see the results", was never entirely satisfied with the accomplishments of his lighter, the theater painter Otto Stoeger, who was often quite desperate. He demanded the impossible even from the technicians. He ordered the stage technician and director Friedrich Brandt, for example, at one point to construct a flying maschine in the shape of a peacock-fanned chariot in which one could fly over the alpine lake. Just as he had his Royal Theatre stage equipped with the most modern lighting and transformation techniques, he always had his old-fashioned looking vehicles and castles fitted out with the most recent technical innovations available. It is characteristic that he mediated an order from the Bavarian government for the generally unacknowledged inventor of the submarine, Wilhelm Bauer. "Hunding's Hut", built in 1876 in the woods near Linderhof, is another example for a stage design set against a natural background.[20] It is a chamber built of roughly worked logs like the decoration from the first act of "Walküre". It was modelled, though, on Christian Jank's design made for the Munich première and not on the Bayreuth decoration. With his great love of trees the King himself almost certainly chose the gnarled trunk around which the chamber, as called for by the design, was supposed to be built. Since Linderhof was surrounded by beech wood, it was only to be expected that the choice would fell on a beech tree to which minor adjustments were then made. "Double beech with a covering of ash wood" note the building plans. In later years the King liked to retreat here to read in loneliness on his bedstead covered in bear furs. He is said to have enlivened his reading with a tableau vivant of his servants posing at a "mead drinking-bout in the old Germanic style". From as early on as 1864, before composition on the tetralogy was even completed, Ludwig had had the "Nibelung Hall" of his Munich residence decorated with Michael Echter's frescos depicting scenes from the operas. Apart from this and the occasional staging of living pictures, Ludwig did not need to have any further stage sets built in order to transpose himself into the world of the "Ring". Nature, in the form of his beloved mountains which he could avail himself of on his walks and drives in the environs of Neuschwanstein and Linderhof, provided him with the "wild rocky mountains" and the "peak of a rocky mountain", the background sets for the second and third acts of "Walküre", as well as the rest of the landscape scenes from the

"Ring". Just as the King attempted to enhance nature with fireworks or the illumination of waterfalls and scenic performances on the alpine Lake, he also strove for something more with his Royal Theatre stage designs depicting nature. Moving beyond a banal naturalism, he aspired towards "the realization of the highest ideal, an ideal that in a certain sense mirrors nature in a fabulous glimmer"[21], an ideal in which historism meets naturalism.

A further stage set, Gurnemanz's hermitage from the third act of "Parsifal", was built in 1877 near the "Hunding's Hut". In a letter the King made direct reference to his desire to immerse himself in the poetry of "Parsifal" here at the "flowery Good Friday Meadow", which was created by the royal gardener with "patches of lawn decked out with an abundance of flowers". Years before the first performance of "Parsifal" Ludwig pondered about its staging.[22] In 1876 he had Eduard Ille sketch a design for a Holy Grail hall in byzantine style modelled on the Hagia Sophia. He developed the idea for a throne hall at Neuschwanstein based on this Holy Grail Hall. By the time Julius Hofmann completed the final blueprint for the throne hall in 1881, the "Wartburg" that had been designed for the young King had been transformed into Parsifal's "Holy Grail Castle" where the aging King struggles for deliverance. The six canonized kings in the apse are for him intercessors and models for kingship based purely on divine right. Painted for the most part by Wilhelm Hauschild, the hall's frescos portray their deeds, above all those of the Holy Ludwig whom the King also honoured in the chapels of Neuschwanstein and Linderhof. In deviation from the original program the adjoining Minstrel's Hall was supposed to now function as an anteroom for the throne hall and was decorated in 1883/1884 with wall paintings based on Wolfram von Eschenbach's "Parzival". In the Minstrel's Arcade Parzival appears as the King of the Holy Grail, opposite his son Lohengrin sets off from the Holy Grail Castle, thus bringing us back full circle to the Swan Knight theme at the beginning of Neuschwanstein's origins.

The throne hall at Neuschwanstein, scheduled to be completed in the year Ludwig II died, never held a throne. It is only byzantine project of the King's which was ever implemented. As early as 1869 Dollmann and later, towards the end of the King's life, Hofmann had designed large-scale byzantine palaces for him but they had never been built. As at Herren-chiemsee, though in a different form, the palaces were conceived as manifestations of his kingship as a divine right. One of the King's last projects was planned for the late gothic robber knight castle at Falken-stein. Based on a initial design by Christian Jank, the project was taken over by the Prince von Thurn und Taxis' chief surveyor Max Schultze from Regensburg in 1884. Plans called for a bedchamber in the style of the throne hall at Neuschwanstein and conceived of as a holy shrine. As the money began to run out the King insisted on this one last room, whose proportions grew ever grander over time, being completed. The last sur-viving document is a sectional drawing by Eugen Drollinger which was still lying on the drawing-board when the news of the King's death was announced.

The same King who jubilated about the future festivals to be held in Sem-per's planned but never built theatre on the hills overlooking the Isar:[23] "Thousands will pilgrim from far and near to the national festival", would later in his life have "Parsifal" staged in a private performance. The private performances,[24] at which guests were as equally unwelcome as at Ludwig's castles, demonstrate most obviously the King's turning his back on art for the benefit of the general public and in favour of art for his own private consumption. At the same time the King intermittently forswore Wagner and the medieval world in favour of "other ideals" which had also pre-occupied the King since early youth. In his correspondence with the com-poser the King did not allude to these ideals of which his "divine friend" had no comprehension. King Ludwig himself set up the very original theatre program with performances generally taking place in the months of April, May and November in order to make his much hated "forced stays" in the residence city endurable. As of 1872 two hundred and nine private performances altogether took place, among them, starting in 1878, forty-four operas. Not only Richard Wagner's operas, but also works by Giuseppe Verdi, Meyerbeer, Auber and others were performed. French his-tory during the age of the Bourbons remained, though, a main theme. The King, for whom daily reading was a highly pleasurable pursuit – "a pleasure that I almost indulge in too frequently and cannot do without even when driving in my carraige through the most gorgeous mountain valleys"[25] –, knew all the historical works, memoirs and travel descriptions from this period and had any plays in French or German sent to him. His favourite play was Albert Emil Brachvogel's "Narzifl", the only work to be performed a total of twelve times, in each case on May 9th, the anniversary of Louis XV's death. The King had the play, which had been a regular feature of the general theatre program for some time, revamped. Year after year another guest actress was brought to Munich to play the role of Pompadour while Ernst von Possart always played the title role. The actor and later theatre director cultivated a correspondence with the King concerning the correct interpretation of his role on the basis of his historical and art history studies.

If a historical theme struck the King as especially suitable, he would have one of his "royal poets", August Fresenius, Hermann von Schmid, Ludwig Schneegans or Karl von Heigel, put it into dramatic form. The overriding principle of the King was historical accuracy and he would even want to be shown the historical source material used by the poets. On occasion he even demanded that only engravings be allowed to serve as authentic picture source material for the stage action. He ordered some plays to be written obviously only in order to be able to view certain scenes on stage. Individual stage designs would be constructed without any correlation to the play itself and presented before or after the performance; in the case of the grotto at Linderhof often with changing lights. The stage designers – Angelo Quaglio, Christian Jank and Heinrich Döll – also had to do historical research and were often sent to the relevant locations, notably Versailles but also to Reims to view the cathedral portrait of the "Maid of Orléans" or to Switzerland for "Wilhelm Tell". The only other person to make the same effort to stage historically authentic scenes was the Duke of Meiningen who occasionally exchanged correspondence with Ludwig. Otherwise, even the larger-scale stages at that period simply assembled a lot of their decorations from available stores.

At one point in time there were plans to transfer operations for the private performances to Linderhof palace. In view of his strained finances in 1876, however, Ludwig gave up his plans for a theatre project at the palace and instead had the less expensive Round Temple built. Nonetheless, the King wanted the historical figures of the French court, who appeared again and again in the private performances, to at least be present in the form of pastel painted portraits. The first ground-plan for the extension of the "King's Cottage", sketched by the Master of the Horse Hornig according to the King's specifications, already calls for cabinets along the sides to ensconce the portraits. "Do everything you can to obtain a picture of the Marquise de Créqui ... I absolutely need a pastel portrait of her for Linderhof, I am now reading her very interesting 7 volume memoirs"[26], the King wrote to Privy Councillor Düfflipp in 1871. Naturally, Pompadour was included in the King's collection of pastel portraits which he rearranged several times. He even gave orders that the painter Heigel "be supplied with a sample of the dress worn by Fräulein Ziegler in the play 'Narzifl' in order to be able to reproduce it accurately in the picture".[27] In the dining room with its "wave-the-magic-wand" trapdoor table Ludwig could be alone even at meals times and believe himself to be in the company of the characters represented by the pastel portraits in the adjoining cabinet. It is therefore no wonder that he himself on occasion wanted to wear the costumes designed by Seitz for the private performances. The order: "in all discretion His Honour desires, only for a short time, that a number of hats and a beautiful, complete costume of the late Louis XV period be sent to him as soon as possible from the theater"[28] speaks for such an assumption as well as the fact that an ostentatious outfit of Louis XV's was sold as part of the King Ludwig's estate.

Theatre Director Franz Seitz, the costume designer for the Royal Theatre, was involved as early as 1869 in the completion of Ludwig's rooms at his Munich residence. He provided not only suitable costumes for the King, but also a number of interior decoration designs for Linderhof, along with the stage painter Christian Jank who was also a specialist for the rococo interiors of the private performances. Designed by the architect Georg Dollmann in cooperation with theatre painters,[29] the palace in its construction is an unmistakable creation of historism and, just like Neuschwanstein, is associated with certain stage design ideas. What was planned and executed here as the best of handicrafts – the carvings by the sculptor Philipp Perron, stuccowork by Theobald Bechler – is the quite independent rococo style of Ludwig II. While its roots, from folk art to Bavarian late rococo still viable in the 19th century, on occasion break to

137

the surface, the inexhaustible fantasy of the style outstrips its various models. This can be seen, for example, in the Mirror Hall which takes up the motif of the mirrored cabinet so characteristic of German 18th century palaces. This special style developed for Ludwig was even later able to quote certain specific rococo models without simply turning out pale copies. An example is the Hubertus Pavillon at Linderhof which was designed by Julius Hofmann in 1885 and modelled on Cuvilliés' Amalienburg as well as the last addition to the bedchamber at Linderhof which Eugen Drollinger was supposed to model after Cuvilliés' bedchamber in the "Rich Rooms" of the residence. Even the patterns for the mirror frames and the lamps, which were made by a porcelain manufacturer in Meiflen specializing in traditional rococo designs, had to be sketched in Munich and approved of by the King.

The main motif of the private performances – the court life and art of the Bourbons – was also mirrored by the picture program for the palace. The King oversaw the implementation of this program with the same critical eye with which he inspected the designs for a special porcelain dinner service with scenes from the period of Louis XIV and Louis XV earmarked for Linderhof. In a note on the margin of a design by Joseph Watters for a coffee pot depicting "Louis XIV et Molière", for example, is written: "The picture should be better executed, specifically the bedstead should be treated in greater detail, the faces made more noble and altogether the copperplate engraving at hand be more closely adhered to".[30] Time after time it is the figure of Louis XIV that "should be portrayed more nobly and more imposingly in his posture and in his whole personal appearance".[31] Formal mistakes were also criticized, such as the perspective or the colours. There was no room for independent artists at Linderhof and, taken as such, their creations are just as second-rate as the paintings at Neuschwanstein. Nonetheless, they must be seen within the larger picture of the King's desire to create an all-encompassing, collective work of art. It also includes the park completed by the Director of the Royal Gardens Effner by the autumn of 1877. It is beyond doubt one of the most important pleasure-grounds of the 19th century with its strict composition at the axial of the castle giving way to an expansive landscape garden which melts into the surrounding mountain woods. While at Neuschwanstein the surrounding mountains determined the placement of the windows, the gardens at Linderhof play a paramount focal role. The King, for example, had a view of the cascade from his bed. Just like the landscaped gardens of the 18th century with their different "fabriques", Neuschwanstein and Linderhof emerge as the main focal fulcrums for Ludwig II's gigantic nature park with its royal mountain lodges[32] and its various planned and implemented projects, stretching from Garmisch over Plan Lake to the foot of Falkenstein in eastern Allgäu.

The King would frequently, usually by night, travel through this realm in golden splendid carriages and sleighs to match his castles. They were designed by the Royal Theatre Director Franz Seitz and built by the Royal Carriage Manufacturers Franz Gmelch and Johann Michael Mayer.[33] The grooms, the Master of the Horse and the King himself as well would wear costumes in the corresponding style. R. Wenig painted a picture of one of the King's sleigh rides from his castle at Neuschwanstein over Schützensteig to Linderhof in around 1880. Against the background of the snowy night landscape, golden cupids hold a magically bright – thanks to an electric battery – shining crown over the King who appeared immune to the cold even on drives lasting hours. Already in possession of the large-scale gala carriage and the smaller gala carriage which could be converted into a sleigh in winter, Ludwig dreamed of acquiring a new vehicle in 1873: "Last night His Majesty dreamed", as the report of a lackey reads, "of a beautiful gala carriage ... in the middle jinn held up a crown, another crown that could be seen at the front of the carriage was also held up by jinn. The whole carriage was fantastically carved, palms, jinn and amourettes decorated the whole vehicle and it looked as if the body of the carriage was being held up by jinn ...".[34] A sketch and a small-scale model are all that are left of the King's dream. Like many of his later coach and sleigh projects, it never came to be built.

He had another dream, the biggest of his life, which he wanted to fulfill: to build a new Versailles. Originally planned for Linderhof under the codename "Meicost-Ettal" (an anagram for "l'état c'est moi"), the foundation stone for the new castle, after years of painstaking preparations, could be laid on Herren Island in Lake Chiem in 1878.[35] That a copy of an equestrian statue of Louis XIV is standing in the vestibule on the very threshold of Linderhof, is indicative of the fact that it meant more to him than simply a token of historical reminiscence. Ludwig, namely, could trace his name back to that of the Bourbons: his godfather was his grandfather King Ludwig I whose own godfather was in turn none other than King Louis XVI of France (tr. note: Ludwig is the German version of the French/English name Louis). Plans for a new Versailles along with his journey to a defeated France in 1874 could have given rise to political misinterpretations by the nationalists of Bismarck's German Empire which Ludwig, albeit against his will, had helped found. Nonetheless, though the King viewed "Meicost-Ettal" as a monument to Ludwig XIV as a sort of distantly related godfather, he did not see it primarily as an monument to a French king. It was rather a monument to the creator and unique embodiment of royal absolutism which had been rocked to its foundations by the executions of Louis XVI and Marie Antoinette whose deaths had always been particularly shocking for Ludwig. While the "Royal Villa" at Linderhof was planned as a relatively modest sized apartment for the King, "Meicost-Ettal", which grew to ever larger and larger proportions in Georg Dollman's plans, was designed to act as a kind of reincarnation of royal absolutism. Denied unlimited powers in real life, Ludwig could "remember" what it was like to live as a real King when he strolled through the vacant rooms, devoid of irksome courtiers, far removed from the "bourgeois blues" of the 19th century.

Ludwig II's final plans foresaw the New Castle as being built on the same grand scale as the original Versailles. Even in the light of the 19th century love of copies, his vision of an imitation of such enormous dimensions is without parallel. In contrast to the more common imitations of sculpture and pictures, it is an unique experiment which can serve to illustrate all the possibilities as well as the limitations of architectural imitations. The model for the copy must be understood as an intrinsic whole, though, in fact the irregularities of Versailles – began by Louis XIII, enlarged and extended in a number of different phases by Louis XI, with changes being made right into the 19th century – often made it difficult for Ludwig II to reconcile the actual building with his vision of the Versailles of Louis XIV. This forced the creation of a distinct "style in the spirit of the same". Nonetheless, there is no denying the spirit of the 19th century even in the

140

few seemingly closely copied parts. After often being established with some difficulty, the historical model frequently then simply served as a jumping off point for the actual construction which adhered to a design plan developed on the basis of its own logical rules. While the overall ground-plan over time came to more and more closely resemble that of Versailles, the typically 19th century predilection for strict symmetry tended to act as a regulating element. For the outer facade the King could demand that his architect Georg Dollmann make an exact replica of the famous garden facade from Versailles, while the courtyard facade of the castle, dating back to the time of Louis XIII, was supposed to be redesigned in the style of Louis XIV. Inseparably bound to the concept of Versailles, the park, as planned by Carl von Effner, was conceived as more than just a copy of the existing grounds. Fitted up with a real functioning Latona fountain, it was rather to rise again in all its "original glory"; an added enhancement being its unique island location at the point where the Great Canal flows into the lake. Long before laying the foundation stone for Herrenchiemsee, Ludwig had had the castle and park of Versailles brought to life on the stage; specifically in "Der Weg zum Frieden (The Path to Peace)" written according to his specifications by Ludwig Schneegans (première May 6th, 1874), in other private performances, as well as with stage designs featuring the "Salon de l'oeil de boeuf", the bedroom, the counselling room and the mirror gallery. Proof that the King perceived the palace itself as a stage-set, a back-drop of sorts, is his order to have important historical figures from the court of Louis XIV, "dressed in authentic portrait-like costumes from the era"[36] placed peeping out the windows of the north side-wing before the outside finish had even been completed.

By September 1884 work had progressed to the point that the King was able to order a general "illumination" of the island at the hands of Karl Lautenschläger, the Royal Theatre's maschinist, and Alois Zettler, a pioneer in electrical engineering. They constructed what is probably the world's first electrically illuminated "Son et Lumière". Basically, it demonstrates the same principle of transferring stage effects to a setting in the "open nature" as also evidenced by the grotto at Linderhof. Back-drops were simply set up in places the royal gardener had not yet gotten around to filling up with the huge flower arrangements that arrived by the freight train load from Holland and which it was his job to put in place. It is presumably in this same spirit that the King requested the planting of a large avenue of imitation trees extending a half kilometre into the lake and held in place by anchored floats. Despite considerable technical difficulties, Lautenschläger and Zettler managed to install an electric network on the island supplied with power by three steam machines. The network powered the batteries for the colour floodlights attached to poles and trestles which were even connected to each other via the telephone to ease communication between the lighters. The King was highly gratified by the performances lasting from midnight to two in the morning and appointed Zettler to the position of – First Royal Illuminator".

As with the Minstrel's Hall at Neuschwanstein, plans for Herrenchiemsee from the start called for two adjoining rooms which were the actual motive behind having the palace built in the first place: the state bedchamber and the mirror gallery. From the first design of a small Versailles confined to a single wing to the full-fledged project, the "Chambre de Parade" remained on the east side adjoined to the mirror gallery on the west side, as is the case at Versailles. Together they form the middle axis which extends along the east-west axis of the garden all the way into the canal. Honoured as the Holy of the Holies by the court ceremonials of royal absolutism, the chamber, unlike Ludwig's bedroom at Linderhof, cannot serve as his sleeping place – it remains reserved for Louis XIV. For the latter born Bavarian King the room seemed to be a "menetekel for the impotency of his own kingship".[37] Interestingly enough, the state bedchamber is anything but a copy of the much more modest "Chambre de Parade" at Versailles. By the time Julius Hofmann (Dollmann's successor as the superintendent for construction at Herrenchiemsee as of 1884) completed the final version of the room, the King's desire to have it furnished and decorated in the most splendid style possible was without its equal even in the late 19th century, with a price tag of more than 384,000 florins. Costly textiles had been ordered for the state bedchamber as early as 1875, three years before building on the castle had even begun. The Munich studio of Jörres and Bornhauser spent seven years alone working on the curtains for the grandiloquent bed.

In the drama "Das Alter eines groflen Königs (The Age of a Great King)" from Lockroy and Arnould (première November 7th, 1873), the King had first seen scenes set in the state bedchamber as well as the mirror gallery on stage. While a sense of complete illusion was the only thing that mattered for him as far as staging went, at Herrenchiemsee the King insisted on a complete true-to-scale copy, including the adjoining corner rooms, the Peace Hall and the War Hall. He reprimanded Dollmann for "being guilty of high-handed arbitrariness" due to a discrepancy of only eight feet in the sum of the total measurements.[38] A colossal sized copy of the plafond could only be accomplished by a whole group of "conscientious painters" who were sent to Versailles in 1879 to "intensively imbue the character of the paintings there".[39] After the King had inspected the finished gallery at the end of September 1881, he noticed on hand from a copperplate engraving that the position of two pictures had been changed: "Since such a mix-up could occur with two paintings, His Majesty assumes that this is possible in other cases as well, which would be something dreadful for His Majesty and a thing His Majesty could never forgive".[40] The King was also not completely satisfied with the colours for the mirror gallery. Being a night owl, he generally saw his rooms lit up at night and loved to see surprising light effects similar to those in a theatre. Especially for his favourite colour blue, but for reds and greens as well, he demanded strong, brilliant tones while he generally didn't want anything to do with yellow at all. Blue was the colour his mother chose for him when he was still a child while his brother Otto's colour was red. "The coloration in the large gallery, the War Hall and the Peace Hall is much too pale", is the complaint in a report addressed to the Privy Councillor Bürkel, "His Majesty has already had occasion to declare that His Majesty cannot stand pale tones."[41]

The stairwell of the south wing, a replica of the "Escalier des Ambassadeurs" pulled down in Versailles in 1752, acted as an anteroom for the other state rooms which were added to the mirror gallery in 1883. The reconstruction, modelled on contemporary engravings, is nonetheless a typical work of the 19th century with its modern glass roof allowing the bright sunlight to shine on the lively colours of the marble and the white stucco. In keeping with pictures painted in the style of the Makart period, the stairwell was transformed into a grove of lilies and roses during the King's sojourn. Adjoining the large apartment in the style of Louis XIV, another smaller apartment in the style of Louis XV was built. It is completely in the tradition of the rococo style developed for Ludwig II at Linderhof and has little in common with the corresponding apartment of Louis XV on the upper floor of the north wing at Versailles. Aside from the rooms by Julius Hofmann, the Blue Salon and the dressing-room designed by Franz Paul Stulberger count as the most original rooms of the apartment. Covered with carvings of festooned flowers and birds, the mirrors transform the rooms into an endless series of arbours. In contrast to the red state bedchamber, the small bedroom used by Ludwig II, like his bedrooms at Neuschwanstein and Linderhof, is decorated in the King's favourite colour. Otto Stoeger, responsible for the illumination of the grotto at Linderhof, experimented for a year and a half before the King was satisfied with the lighting: A blue globe was to bath the room in a constant blue colour.

When work on the building had to be discontinued in 1885 the north side-wing, torn down later in 1907, was still in an unfinished state and the south side-wing had not been built beyond the foundation. Nonetheless, Herrenchiemsee has not remained an "unfulfilled dream". Ludwig's concept of Versailles incorporated only a certain group rooms, almost all of which were successfully completed. The gigantic caves of rough brickwork encasing these rooms didn't play a role in the King's vision and were therefore left open in the design. Ludwig complained about the rough brickwork on his first visit in 1881 which he felt could have at least been temporarily covered over in the rooms directly adjoining the bedroom. For the present-day visitor who steps from the splendour of the show rooms into the unfinished north stairwell, though, the rough brickwork appears as intriguing as a spectator's first visit backstage to the world behind the stage.

In the vestibule at Herrenchiemsee, as well as at the Moorish Kiosk at Linderhof, the peacock, one of Ludwig's favourite animals, is depicted. Within the realm of the swan, Ludwig's other favourite animal, it only appears on the periphery in the arched curves of the Minstrel's Hall as a symbol of bliss and immortality. Putting Wagner and the Middle Ages to the side, the peacock links the other two major areas of interest determining Ludwig's world view: the age of the Bourbons and the world of the orient. Familiar to him through his books, the East held, as it did for many of his contemporaries, an immense attraction. Among all the possible areas of domination suggested to the King by the archivist Löher, it is not by chance that, along with the valleys of Hindu Kush, Egypt and Afghanistan appeared most acceptable "primarily for the reason ... because the development of a splendid sovereignty only seems possible in these lands".[42] Even Wagner planned an opera with an oriental motif, "Die Sieger (The Victor)", whose implementation the King hoped for in vain: "In a fascinating book about India, Brahmanism and Buddhism to my joyful surprise I found a simple, and for that very reason, a very moving and touching story which you would want to use as material for 'The Victor' ... It will one day be counted as one of your most glorious works, believe me. India and Buddhism have an indescribable attraction for me, stirring desire and supreme delight".[43]

Made famous by its tremendous success during the World's Fair in Paris, Jules Massenet's opera "The King of Lahore" is also set in India. After a dress rehearsal in 1879 the King demanded the staging of two private performances. In the following years Jank, Döll and Quaglio also provided lavish settings for a number of private performance operas with oriental motifs, among them Mozart's "Magic Flute" (1879), Karl Goldmark's "The Queen of Saba" (1880) and Weber's "Oberon" (1881). The King even charged Franz Wüllner with a complete reworking of the latter. He was especially taken with the decoration for David's "Lala Rookh". He had a painting of the Kashmir valley made for this opera in 1876 – a model still exists – which he even wanted to have rendered in the grotto at Linderhof to replace the picture of Tannhäuser.[44] He also had Karl Heigel translate and rework Kalidasa's Indian drama "Sakuntala". A second work of his as well, the Indian fairy tale "Urvasi", which was staged at the last private performance on May 12th, 1885. The King had commanded that the decoration be designed "not on a pattern but modelled on authentic, true-to-nature pictures of the Himalaja Mountains".[45] The stage technician Lautenschläger's report is characteristic of the King's decoration wishes which placed equal value on "authentic" nature and "authentic" historical places of interest: "The King desired that the jungle be animated with birds of paradise, parrots, singing birds, elephants and other types of animal marching past him. I had already finished the plan and the drawing was presented to His Majesty on his return from on outing on which he happened to have seen some 'grazing stags'. His Majesty then wanted to see the peaceful image of the grazing deer in the Indian jungle. The upshot was that the grazing stags were added to a busy picture of the jungle." After the conclusion of the performance to everyone's complete satisfaction Lautenschläger received the following message: "that the King remarked: 'Herr Lautenschläger lets the animals starve in the Indian woods. Animals don't just take walks in the woods, they use their sojourn to look for food. Lautenschläger shouldn't just have the animals go for a walk at the second performance. Furthermore, the Indian sun whose rays brighten up the woods must be more strongly manifested and generate another, more lively play of colours'".[46]

The King also wanted to transpose the winter garden built on the roof of the north tract (Festsaalbau) of his Munich residence to the same Indian fairy-tale world. With its daring construction of glass and iron, it far surpasses the old winter garden of his father Maximilian at the southeast corner of the residence. Like the iron palm house of King Friedrich Wilhem IV on Peacock Island near Potsdam, it is part of the so-called palm house tradition and an important exponent of 19th century architecture. Against the back-drop of the Himalajas painted by Christian Jank, the Director of the Royal Gardens Effner had tropical vegetation grouped around a lake. Ludwig's enthusiasm for such jungle plant arrangements was not at all unusual at a time when tropical plants and "oriental" furnishings enjoyed immense popularity and the well-known "Makart" bouquet decorated the homes of better-off citizens. Ever since his visit to the World's Fair of 1867 in Paris the King had developed a taste for "oriental" buildings. Early on he began to transplant such structures to the Bavarian mountains which occasionally took on the contours of the Kashmir valley with the Himalaja as back-drop in his imagination. His first building project in an oriental style was the Schachen hunting lodge built in 1870. Though on the outside a simple mountain hut made of wood, on the inside it was a luxuriously furnished turkish *salle*. "Wearing traditional turkish attire the

King would sit here reading," Luise von Kobell reports, "while a pack of servants dressed as moslems lounged about on cushions and rugs smoking tobacco and lapping up mocha, as the royal Lord had commanded them to. He would often look up from his book to glance around the stylish group with a superior smile. Peacock fans being waved through the air and the the pungent haze from the incense stove helped to complete the illusion".[47] Although Ludwig II already had kiosks in his winter garden and in Schloss Berg, he bought another, similar looking pavillon from Castle Zbirow in Bohemia in 1876 and had it set up at Linderhof. This Moorish Kiosk was originally built for the 1867 World's Fair in Paris which the King visited on his first trip to the French capital. Created by the architect Karal von Diebitsch, the focal point of the kiosk is the peacock throne designed by Franz Seitz and made in Paris.[48] The architect Dollmann was sent to the 1878 World's Fair in Paris to report on the different oriental houses which were all the fashion in Europe at the time. Among houses from Algeria, Persia, Egypt and China, he finally chose the most beautiful, the Moroccan House, for the King. It was put up the very same year at Linderhof where "His Majesty would like to use the same to read for a few undisturbed hours".[49] Other oriental projects such as the Moorish Hall at Castle Neuschwanstein never came to be built. After the King had acquired different sketches of the imperial winter palace in Beijing, Julius Hofmann designed a "Chinese" palace in 1886. It was supposed to be built on the lonely Plan Lake. There the King, who was very interested in Chinese court ceremony, would have been able to give himself over to playing out the role of the autocratic sovereign for the last time.[50]

In the age of Historicism Ludwig, in contrast to builders of previous centuries, was able to choose not only the location and theme for his projects but the style as well. To the Neo-Baroque style favoured by his father and grandfather, he added supplementary rococo elements popular in Germany since the design of the Liechtenstein Palace in Vienna and in France since the time of the Louis-Philippe style. He turned from the Neo-Gothic style of his father to the Neo-Romanesque style of Neuschwanstein and with the Romantics and their followers shared a love for everything oriental. His grandfather's enthusiasm for Greece and Italy, he never even visited the latter once, left Ludwig cold – "the lands of Hellas scorched by the burning sun would rather repel than attract me", he wrote at one time to Wagner.[51] He built an architectural copy of Versailles and not architectural copies based on Greek and Italian models like his grandfather. Ludwig I as well knew how to succeed in having his often highly individual design ideas carried out against the opposition of his architects. While Ludwig I endeavoured to parley with the artists, his grandson developed his ideas in lonely isolation consulting solely his own artistic sensibilities. Through his court officials he would then simply passed on his orders to the artists, orders which often dictated form and content down to the tiniest details. In this sense Ludwig II was not just a building owner but a creator of buildings, who could not tolerate any idiosyncrasy on the part of his often merely skillful but not very original painters, sculptors and poets. Wagner was one the very few artists for whom Ludwig was an ideal patron, perhaps because the King was more of a music lover than a music expert in any way and stood in uncritical awe of Wagner's poetical works. Semper also knew how to win over the young King to his conception for a festival theatre – without a doubt the most important theatre project of the second half of the 19th century which ran aground due to Wagner's ambiguous attitude more than to any trouble made by the King's circle.

As one of the most active patrons of buildings in the Historicism style, Ludwig II's primary concern was for historic truth, determined on the basis of his own scientific and literary studies. Even in those cases where the King simply wished for copies to be made, though, his art demonstrates the unmistakable character of Historicism as an independent form of artistic achievement. In the actual implementation a style planned as Louis XV, for example, would be transformed into Ludwig II's unmistakable rococo style, often even outdoing the design plans. In connection with the 19th century style of naturalism it is interesting to Note here the occasional, astonishing foreshadowing of Art nouveau. This is not just true of the products designed by Adolph Seder and Franz Brochier, whose craft works are also characterized by the idiosyncratic brightness of their colours.[52] The newest technical innovations were applied, for example, the use of metal casting for the decorations and figures of the roof-construction. Even if only for the sake of creating a illusion, astonishingly "modern" solutions for problems were found, such as plate-glass for windows and the sliding door of the winter garden at Neuschwanstein. At the same time, nonetheless, Ludwig's building projects helped to keep up the traditional craftsmanship of the 18th century longer in Bavaria than anywhere else in Germany. For example, Franz Seitz' son and coworker Rudolf Seitz was the first head of the restauration workshops, which later developed into the workshops of the Land Office for the Protection of National Treasures. The sizeable orders of the King – for the royal cabinetmaker Pössenbacher, for the embroidery makers Jörres and Bornhauser, for the royal silversmiths Harrach and Wollenweber, for the jewellers Merk and Rath, for the locksmiths Kölbel and Moradelli, for the Royal Glassworks Zettler, and for the Royal Artworks Mayer, among others, – made Munich one of Europe's most important centers for artcrafts, able to hold its own against even Vienna and Paris to which the King also sent orders.

While Maximilian II and Ludwig I built primarily for the public, Ludwig II thought of his castles as so exclusively his own that he could even consider having them destroyed after his death. Though the King showed considerable political acme at the beginning of his career, he gradually lost interest in politics to the point that in 1870 he gave orders – not to speak of politics anymore without Majesty asking about it".[53] His interest and an enormous amount of activity was directed towards developing his art instead. His stage productions and his castles, though, were more than just a make-believe world he retreated to in protest against the bourgeois world which could not comprehend him. They were his life, a life in which dream and reality were an entity and past history became presence, not just in the theatre. Contrary to the general opinion that Ludwig ruined the state finances with his projects, they were all financed by his cabinet treasury. Considering the defeat in 1866 which weakened the sovereignty of his kingship, there is reason for his lack of interest and willingness to invest energy in political questions, two traits he otherwise amply demonstrated in connection with his art projects.[54] Life lost all meaning for him when the debts of the cabinet treasury forced him to stop building. The ruin of "the only true King of the century", a man in despair of his job as a monarch in a constitutional monarchy, was not "mental illness" which only served as a pretext for certain political circles. Rather, it was his despair at no longer being grudged the privilege of creating his art with its many-layered world view, his despair at not being left alone in "ideal-monarchial-poetical loneliness"[55] on the stage of his life.

Notes

1. For a comprehensive presentation of the King's artistic endeavours see Michael Petzet, König Ludwig II. und die Kunst, Catalogue of the 1968 Exhibition in the Munich Residence; in addition Michael Petzet/Werner Neumeister, Die Welt des Bayerischen Märchenkönigs, Ludwig II. und seine Schlösser, Munich 1980. – M. Petzet, Ludwig II and the Arts, in: Wilfrid Blunt, The Dream King, London 1970. – Concerning the interrelationship between architecture and the theatre, see M. Petzet, L'architecture comme dècor du théatre dans Part deLouis II. Roi de Bavière, in: Gazette des Beaux-Arts 1970, p 209–236.
2. For a complete documentation of Wagner's "model performances" see Detta and Michael Petzet, Die Richard-Wagner-Bühne König Ludwigs II., Munich 1970.
3. Heinrich Kreisel, Die Schlösser Ludwigs II. von Bayern, Darmstadt 1955, p 19. – See also H. Kreisel, Ludwig II. als Bauherr, in: Oberbayerisches Archiv, Bd. 87, Munich 1965, p 69–87. – Kreisel also established the Ludwig II museum at Herrenchiemsee (first official guide 1926) and wrote new editions of the official guides for the King's castles (Herrenchiemsee 1929, Linderhof 1930, Neuschwanstein, 1933).
4. Tagebuch-Aufzeichnungen von Ludwig II, König von Bayern, ed. Edir Grein (Riedinger), Schaan/Liechtenstein, 1925, p 3.
5. Heinrich Kreisel, Schloß Hohenschwangau, Munich 1953, p 5.
6. Compare Petzet, Richard Wagner Bühne (Note 2), p 134.
7. Letter from Ludwig II to Cosima von Bülow, Hohenschwangau, August 29th, 1867. Geheimes Hausarchiv 55/5/54 m.
8. Letter from Ludwig II to Richard Wagner, May 13th, 1868. Otto Strobel, König Ludwig II und Richard Wagner, Briefwechsel in fünf Bänden, Karlsruhe 1936–39, Bd. II, pp 224–25.
9. Quote from Kreisel, Die Schlösser Ludwig II's (Note 3), p 72.
10. Hornig to Privy Councillor Bürkel, Hohenschwangau, February 2nd, 1880, with a simple sketch by Hornig. Handschriftenabteilung der Bayer. Staatsbibliothek, Bürkeliana 38.
11. For more information about Neuschwanstein's picture program see Sigrid Russ, Die Ikonographie der Wandmalerien im Schloß Neuschwanstein, dissertation, Heidelberg 1974, as well as S. Russ, Neuschwanstein, der Traum eines Königs, Munich 1983.
12. Letter from Welker to Privy Councillor Bürkel, April 5th, 1879. Korr. Bürkel (Korrespondenz des Hofsekretärs Ministerialrat Ludwig von Bürkel, 1879–1882 in the archive of the King Ludwig II Museum).
13. Letter from Mayr to Privy Councillor Bürkel, Hohenschwangau, February 3rd, 1882. Korr. Bürkel.
14. Letter from Hartmann to Privy Councillor Düfflipp, Berg, May 28th 1869. Korr. Düfflipp (Korrespondenz des Hofsekretärs Hofrat Lorenz von Düfflipp, 1869–1878, in the archive of the King Ludwig II Museum).
15. Catalogue 1968 (Note 1), No. 193–198, 206–214.
16. For a history of the building of Neuschwanstein see Kreisel (Note 3); Petzet (Note 1) and Petzet, Schloß Neuschwanstein, official guide, Munich 1970; Russ (Note 11); Jutta Tschoeke, Neuschwanstein, Planungs- und Baugeschichte eines königlichen Burgbaus im ausgehenden 19. Jahrhundert, dissertation, Munich 1975.
17. For an interpretation of the use of the stage sets of the Munich performances of Wagner's operas in the building design of Neuschwanstein see the chapters "Lohengrin" and "Tannhäuser" in Neuschwanstein, in: Petzet, Richard Wagner-Bühne (Note 2), pp 133 ff.
18. Letter from Lutz to Privy Councillor Düfflipp, May 16th, 1867. Geheimes Hausarchiv 55/5/54 d.
19. For information about the grotto at Linderhof see Petzet, Richard Wagner-Bühne (Note 2), pp 140 ff. and the chapter –Die Venusgrotto" in Petzet/Neumeister (Note 1), pp 69 ff.
20. For information about the "Hunding Hut" see Petzet, Richard Wagner-Bühne (Note 2), pp 218 ff.
21. Letter from Ludwig II to Richard Wagner, August 19th, 1865. Strobel (Note 8) I, p 153.
22. For more information about the stage set for "Parsifal" compare Petzet, Richard Wagner-Bühne (Note 2), pp 270 ff.
23. For more information about the Munich festival theatre project (1864/68) see Heinrich Habel, Festspielhaus und Wahnfried, geplante und ausgeführte Bauten Richard Wagners, Munich 1985, pp 20 ff.
24. Kurt Hommel, Die Separatvorstellungen for König Ludwig II von Bayern, Munich 1963. Neither the archival material or the numerous pictorial sources for the decoration of the private performances have been adequately studied. – Compare also the Catalogue 1968 (Note 1), pp 47 ff., No. 386–414.
25. Letter from Ludwig II to Richard Wagner, June 21st, 1873. Strobel (Note 8) III, p 17.

26 Letter from Ludwig II to Privy Councillor Düfflipp, November 2nd, 1871. Korr. Düfflipp.

27 Letter from Walter to Privy Councillor Düfflipp, Linderhof, August 17th 1872. Korr. Düfflipp.

28 Letter from Walter to Privy Councillor Düfflipp, Hohenschwangau, December 30th, 1875. Korr. Düfflipp.

29 For a history of the building of Linderhof see Kreisel (Note 3); Michael Petzet, Linderhof und Herrenchiemsee, in: Bayerland, 68 Jg., Munich 1966, pp 21 ff.; Catalogue 1968 (Note 1), pp 52 ff., No. 415 ff. – For an attempt at a history of Linderhof's planning based on the extensive design material of the King Ludwig II Museum first made available in catalogue form, see Monika Bachmayer, Schloß Linderhof, Architektur, Interieur und Ambiente einer königlichen Villa, dissertation, Munich 1977.

30 Remark on the design, Catalogue 1968 (Note 1), No. 473.

31 Remark on a design of Walter's for a cup, Catalogue 1968 (Note 1), No. 371.

32 For more information about the mountain huts see Karin and Hannes Heindl, Ludwigs heimliche Residenzen am Walchensee: Hochkopf-Herzogstand-Vorderriß, Munich 1974.

33 Heinrich Kreisel, Prunkwagen und Schlitten, Leipzig 1927; Luisa Hager, Marstallmuseum in Schloß Nymphenburg, official guide, Munich 1959: Catalogue 1968 (Note 1), No. 778–813.

34 Letter from Hornig to Privy Councillor Düfflipp, Hohenschwangau, November 16th, 1873, Korr. Düfflipp.

35 For more information about the history of the planning of Herrenchiemsee see Kreisel (Note 3); Hans Gerhard Evans, Herrenchiemsee, in Tod, Macht und Raum, Munich 1939, pp 199–282; M. Petzet, Linderhof und Herrenchiemsee (Note 29); Catalogue 1968 (Note 1), No. 622–777; Alexander Rauch, Schloß Herrenchiemsee, Entstehungsgeschichte und Wesensbestimmung, unpublished dissertation, Munich 1976; 100 Jahre Herrenchiemsee, Sonderheft der Zeitschrift Bayern, 6. Jg. 1978, with a catalogue of picture documentation about how Herrenchiemsee came into being with contributions from Gerhard Hojer (Schloß Herrenchiemsee – Monument des absoluten Königstums) and Alexander Rauch (Königreich vor Sonnenaufgang, Gedanken zu Sinn und Symbolik in der Architektur Schloß Herrenchiemsee). Unfortunately, neither the archival sources nor the extensive design material for Herrenchiemsee have, to date, been studied or published.

36 Memoirs of the painter Carl Schultheiß (1852–1944). Private manuscript.

37 Kreisel, Die Schlösser Ludwigs II (Note 3), p 55.

38 Letter from Welker to Privy Councillor Bürkel, Linderhof, June 1st, 1879. Korr. Bürke.

39 Letter from Hornig to Privy Councillor Düfflipp, Hohenschwangau, August 3rd, 1875. Korr. Düfflipp.

40 Letter from Mayr to Privy Councillor Bürkel, Pürschling, October 18th, 1881. Korr. Bürkel.

41 Letter from Mayr to Privy Councillor Bürkel, Chiemsee, September 29th, 1881. Korr. Bürkel.

42 Report of Bürkel's from 1879. Handschriftenabteilung der Bayer. Staatsbibliothek, Bürkeliana.

43 Letter from Ludwig II to Richard Wagner, June 15th, 1870. Strobel (Note 8) II, p 310.

44 Catalogue 1968 (Note 1) No. 898, illus. p 136; also here No. 822–833: stage set designs for the private performances with "oriental" motifs.

45 Müncher Allgemeine Zeitung from April 25th, 1893, quoted by Hommel (Note 24), p 129.

46 Oppenheim, in: Fränkischer Kurier from July 26th, 1906, No. 377. Adalbert Prinz von Bayern, Als die Residenz noch Residenz war, Munich 1967, pp 320/21.

47 Luise von Kobell, König Ludwig II von Bayern und die Kunst, 2nd edition. Munich 1906, pp 447/48.

48 For designs of the peacock throne and other oriental projects see Catalogue 1968 (Note 1), No. 834–890. – For information about the influence of the world's fair in Paris on Ludwig II's art and the fashion for oriental design see Isabella Fehle, Der Maurische Kiosk in Linderhof von Kral von Diebitsch, ein Beispiel für die Orientmode im 19. Jahrhundert, unpublished dissertation, Munich 1985.

49 Letter from Siegler to Privy Councillor Düfflipp, Schachen, September 29th, 1878. Korr. Düfflipp. – After the King's death the Moroccan House was sold and switched hands several times (most recently in Oberammergau). The Bavarian Castle Administration has recently been able to repurchase it and it will soon be placed on the palace grounds at Linderhof.

50 Kreisel. Die Schlösser Ludwigs II. (Note 3), p 48.

51 Letter from Ludwig II to Richard Wagner, March 1st, 1882. Strobel (Note 8) II, p 233.

52 Catalogue 1968 (Note 1), No. 600–698, 649–651.

53 Letter from Hornig to Privy Councillor Düfflipp, Berg, October 11th, 1870. Korr. Düfflipp.

54 For more information about the narrow limits set on Bavarian politics and its consequences for the King compare Helmut Dotterweich, Ludwig II. zwischen Bismarck und Lohengrin, in: Löwe & Raute No. 9, December 1985/January 1986, pp 7–9.

55 Letter from Ludwig II to Richard Wagner, January 3rd, 1872. Strobel (Note 8) II, p 335.

Franz Merta

The King's Sojourns at his Residences, Castles and Mountain Lodges

Establishing a reliable overview of King Ludwig II's whereabouts at any given time during his reign poses an especially challenging task for the investigative historian when one considers the claim that his own ministers at the time were not always aware of where he might be sojourning. Although initially a seemingly hopeless enterprise, a practically unbroken chain listing his various and numerous residences has been established. The success of this undertaking was ultimately dependent on the volume of routine work with which the King had to deal with on an almost daily basis and whose spurs can be retraced today in the form of official papers, letters, dictations and other written material which have been preserved in historical archives. It was due to the stipulations of the system of constitutional monarchy then in effect that the King had to busy himself with such a large volume of official documents . In particular, the constitutional amendment concerning ministerial responsibilities which became law in 1848, proscribed in detail, not only for the ministers but the King as well, how the practical, day-to-day work of the government was to be transacted. According to this law, the subordinate government agencies needed the signature not only of the appropriate minister, respectively the ministry as a whole, but that of the King as well, in order to be able to implement not only laws and government decrees but also countless minor administrative regulations. Only the King's signature itself could designate royal sanction of an act of government. In addition to these official documents, King Ludwig II also bequeathed to posterity a voluminous correspondence with his two court secretaries. These were his cabinet secretary who was responsible for transacting the King's official business, in particular his dealings with the various ministries, and the court secretary who dealt with the King's private affairs, above all his building projects. These papers consist of letters written either personally by the King or dictated by him to lackeys. Often containing extensive directives for his secretariats, some of these letters bear his personal signature while others, the so-called lackey letters, were only signed by the acting servant. It must be emphasized, however, that these so-called lackey letters were always of a private nature and did not ever deal with official business. Aside from these papers, there is also the last, but certainly not least, huge number of the King's personal letters; his correspondence with Richard Wagner alone fills five printed volumes. The dates and places noted on all these documents provide a reliable source of information concerning the whereabouts of the King at the time he signed them. Assembled together as if they were pieces of a jigsaw puzzle, they offer the possibility of reconstructing King Ludwig II's itinerary or list of consecutive residences by establishing the existence of at least one signed document with date and place for most days during the greater part of his reign.

The following sources were consulted to ascertain this data.

A. *unpublished sources*

1. King Ludwig II's cabinet documents and the court staff documents preserved in the Bavarian Central State Archive, dept. III: Secret Personal Archive. The numerous surviving letters and papers of the King disclose not only the actual locality at which they were written but also contain many references to other sojourns.

2. The registry records of the Bavarian Ministry of War in the Bavarian Central State Archive, dept. IV. War Archive. The advantage of these records is that they catalogue the places of issue at which King Ludwig II rendered his signature, thus making it superfluous to refer back to the numerous individual original documents.

3. The private papers of the two court secretaries Lorenz von Düfflipp and Ludwig von Bürkel. They can be found under *Correspondence Düfflipp* in the Bavarian Administration of State Castles, Gardens and Lakes at Castle Nymphenburg and *Bürkeliana* in the Manuscript Department of the Bavarian State Library in Munich, respectively. Both collections contain numerous instructions from Ludwig II for his court secretaries for the period between roughly 1867 and 1884. As in the case of the King's cabinet documents, they contain references to his whereabouts at different given times.

4. The chronicle of Castle Hohenschwangau in the Wittelsbacher Settlement Foundation at Castle Nymphenburg which documents not only

Ludwig II's sojourns at Castle Hohenschwangau itself, but also contains references to other places of residence.

5. Numerous individual documents from various departments of the Bavarian Central State Archive for those cases in which there was no other alternative for determining the places of issues at which the King rendered his signature.

6. The loss of a number of key collections of personal papers due to the war noticeably complicated the task of establishing Ludwig II's itinerary. Among them were the private papers of the Queen Mother Marie and those of Prince Otto which meant the decrement of numerous letters from Ludwig II. Similarly, the private papers of the Ludwig II's cabinet secretaries A. von Eisenhart and F. von Ziegler containing letters from him could not be brought to light. On the other hand, the heavy losses suffered during the war by the Bavarian Ministry of Justice and the Home Secretary for Church and School Affairs, did not weigh as heavily. Nonetheless, these losses did sometimes result in not being able to determine the place of issue at which the King rendered his signature for the one or other odd day.

B. published sources

1. Gesetzblatt für das Königreich Bayern 1864–1873 (Law Gazette for the Kingdom of Bavaria 1864–1873).

2. Regierungsblatt für das Königreich Bayern 1864–1873 (Government Gazette for the Kingdom of Bavaria 1864–1873).

3. Gesetz- und Verordnungsblatt für das Königreich Bayern 1873 ff. (The Official Law Gazette for the Kingdom of Bavaria 1873 et sequ.).

4. Justizministerialblatt für das Königreich Bayern 1864 ff. (Ministry of Justice Gazette for the Kingdom of Bavaria 1864 et sequ.).

5. Veordnungsblatt des bayerischen Kriegsministeriums 1864 ff. (The Official Gazette of the Bavarian War Ministry 1864 et sequ.).

6. Ministerialblatt für Kirchen- u. Schulangelegenheiten im Königreich Bayern 1865 ff. (The Ministry for Church and School Affairs Gazette for the Kingdom of Bavaria 1865 et sequ.).

7. Amtsblatt des kgl. Staatsministeriums des Inneren. München 1872 ff. (The Official Gazette of the Royal Home Secretary. Munich 1872 et sequ.).

These publications of the various government agencies and ministries informed the public of any decisions sanctioned by the King as long as they did not impingement on the private sphere of any persons concerned in such decisions. As a rule the announcements about such decisions only mentioned the date and not the place of issue at which the royal signature had been rendered, leading to considerable complications in connection with the work for this paper. This is why the appropriate original documents had to be consulted in hundreds of cases in order to determine the place of issue of specific signatures rendered. Locating such original documents was especially difficult in cases where the signature was rendered, for example, in connection with the awarding of medals. Such decorations might be awarded on some special, albeit unnamed occasion, or at various minor affairs to then be cumulated in collective documents. The main criterion for the ordering of these documents is now difficult to determine. Despite these difficulties and the fact that an analysis of the relevant source material in this connection has not been brought to a complete conclusion, the itinerary as it now stands offers a thorough and comprehensive picture of King Ludwig II's sojourns during his reign. Any additional material that might still remain to be examined in detail could only lead to the most minor of modulations; in no way can one expect to see any essential changes in the picture as a whole. This is why a publication of the itinerary can be published without further hesitation at this point.

An examination of the huge glut of Ludwig literature was only marginally useful for the purposes of this paper. Most of the relevant reports of contemporaries, eye-witnesses and the press proved to often be very imprecise, exaggerated and annoyingly or completely inaccurate. They were, for the most part, unreliable and useless. Some so-called "historical truths" could even be exposed as downright lies with the help of the itinerary. An example are the claims made by Ludwig II's "dutiful" court secretaries Ludwig von Düfflipp, A. von Eisenhart and Eisenhart's wife Louise von Kobell,

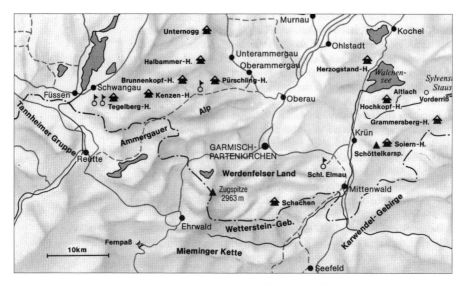

The mountain huts visited by King Ludwig II

about the supposedly eccentric behaviour of the King in connection with the order for mobilization on July 16th, 1870.[1]

An analysis of the itinerary reveals a number of surprising facts about the person and character of King Ludwig II. First of all, there is a clear overview of where and when the King was staying at any one point in time: This is true for his trips as well places he visited regularly.

The itinerary also provides insight about all the places that played an important and consistent role in helping to shape the King's lifestyle. Among these are not only the Residence in Munich and Schloss Berg on Starnberger See, but also Castle Hohenschwangau which his father King Max II had rebuilt, as well as the King's world famous castles Neuschwanstein, Linderhof and Herrenchiemsee. Important are also the eleven mountain huts in the area between Lenggries and Füssen, in part unknown and not all of which have survived to this day. They are as follows: in the northern Karwendel Mountains the mountain huts on Grammersberg (also known as Krametsberg, Kremelsberg, around c. 1540 m); in the Vorderriß at the point where the Riss flows into the Isar and where Ludwig Thoma spent time in his childhood and wrote of in his memoirs;

158

the Sojern Hut near Krün – the highest situated (1610 m), but no longer standing edifice built by the King – with its observation pavillon at the peak of the Schöttelkarspitze (2050 m above sea level) where a mountain cross now stands; on Walchen Lake the mountain huts at Herzogstand (1575 m) and at Hochkopf (1300 m) with its valley station at Altlach; in Wetterstein the well-known Königsschlößchen (= King's Little Castle) on Schachen (1865 m) with its valley station Castle Elmau; in the eastern Ammergauer Alps the mountain huts on Brunnenkopf (1602 m) near Schloss Linderhof, on Pürschling (1565 m) near Unterammgau and in the Halbammer Valley right near the "Wild Hunter" and the Hubertus Chapel with the forest house Unternogg as outpost station at the end of the valley; and finally in the western Ammergauer Alps the Kenzen Hut (also known under the old-fashioned name Kainzen Hut but which has nothing to do with the later famous actor Kainz) and the Tegelberg Hut (1707 m) near Hohenschwangau. The Swiss House near the Post Hotel in Partenkirchen, no longer standing, must also be counted as belonging to this group of the King's residences. Till 1877 Ludwig II would regularly spend a few days here at the end of October and till 1885 would stay overnight here in February on his way back from Hohenschwangau to Munich for the winter season. These mountain huts meant much more to Ludwig than simply places to stay overnight while hunting in the mountains since, unlike his father King Max II and the Prince Regent Luitpold, he didn't hunt. They had for him the character of part-time or, to put it plainly, mountain residences. The huts have no signs pointing out Ludwig's special relationship with them, but for this very reason it must be mentioned that they were the *locus* for shaping, not just general Bavarian history, but art and cultural history as well. On the other hand, the methods applied here were not instrumental in determining the destinations for the many afternoon, evening and night excursions of the King including a number of excursions over the Fern Pass to the inn at Fernstein undertaken as part of his yearly cycle. On such occasions the King would refrain from doing any official business; at the most he might write the infrequent private letter or dictate instructions to his secretaries, for example, at the Swiss House in the Blöckenau, the inn Schluxenwirt, or the post inns in Schlehdorf, Reutee, and Vils.

In its detailed form the itinerary reveals some surprising facts about Ludwig II's work habits with regard to taking care of government business. The official claim that Ludwig II, especially in later years, was not at all involved in everyday government business and left everything to his ministers, and that it is only owing to them that the business of the government could continue to run smoothly without the state suffering any damage, is completely disproved. The running of the government without the cooperation of the King and organized in such a fashion would have been in complete contradiction to the precepts for ministerial responsibility as laid down by the constitution and would, in fact, have amounted to a permanent breach of the same. Despite claims of the opposite from obviously interested sources, there are, on the contrary, thousands of written proofs that demonstrate that the government was run completely in keeping with constitutional law up until June 8th, 1886, the day before the King was arrested. Petitions for proposed measures were submitted to the King for his sanction by either the government as such or the responsible ministries. As a general rule, the King would sanction the measure by virtue of his signature, though, on occasion, he would add a modification or refuse his signature. In the latter case, he would then generally request other suggestions. Alternatively, the King might take the initiative by requesting that suitable proposals be submitted to him by the government or the corresponding ministries. This procedure was in use not only for government acts pertaining to legislation but also for an almost unbelievable amount of simple administrative matters. This was due to a narrow interpretation of the constitutional stipulations regarding matters which were also subject to the King's approval, e.g. the appointment, promotion, transfer, granting of a leave, suspension, marriage and pensioning for the following categories of civil servants: those working for the Ministry of the Interior and the financial administration, high school teachers and university professors, judges and public notaries, foresters, revenue officers and surveyors as well as military officers, diplomats and public health officers. Subject to the King's sanction were also the appointments of parish priests, chaplains, benefices, cathedral curates, bishops, arch-bishops, and cardinals, the changing of surnames, place-names, or parish boundaries, church collection and charity drives on a regional level, grants of citizenship and declarations of majority, the imposition of local beer, malt and flour taxes, pardons and sentence reductions, confirmation of elections for mayors, magistrates and university and academic positions, the granting of orders and court titles, requests for receptions to honour foreign princes and much more of the same. Without any noticeable changes in his working habits, it is proven that till June 8th, 1886 Ludwig II dutifully, if without enthusiasm, discharged all this business for which his grandfather Ludwig I did not want to function as a signature-making machine. During the times he was in residence with his cabinet secretariat – in Munich from around the middle of February till May 10th and the first two weeks of November, in Schloss Berg from May 11th to the end of October and in Hohenschwangau from the middle of November till about the 10th of February – he dispatched the business at hand, day in and day out, not excepting Saturdays or Sundays or even public holidays. During the times he was not in residence with his cabinet secretariat, i.e. during his mountain excursions, his sojourns at Linderhof and Herrenchiemsee as well as his visits to Hohenschwangau during the spring and summer, incoming business was taking care of at regular intervals, usually ever few, at the most every five days. Given this, and in view of the stipulations of the constitution clearly defining the limited participation of the King in the work of the government, there is absolutely no foundation for the accusation that Ludwig II neglected his duties.

(Hsto. 231. 7/3. 69.   Garmisch am 30. Dezember 1868

Koenigliche Hofbau-Intendanz!

Unterthänigste Aufstellung
des
Marktbaumagistrats Garmisch

Betreff:
Die Überhandnahme der Armuth
im Markte Garmisch.

Dem Vernehmen nach sollen in La...
im Linderhof bei Oberammerga...
für Seine Majestaet, unsern
innigstgeliebten Koenig und
Herrn, mehrere größere Baute...
ausgeführt werden.

Angesichts der in ...schreitender
Weise immer mehr überhand neh-
menden Armuth und der Erw...
...tenden Erwerbslosigkeit im
Markte Garmisch wagen wir ...
die Koenigliche Hofbau-Inten...

... mir in paar Kreuzer aufzu-
treiben, um ihren Pflichten gegen
den Staat ꝛc. wenigstens theilweise
nachzukommen, und so kommen
durch die nach und nach in Folge
des vorgeschriebenen Zwangsver-
fahrens abbrechenden Heerden ꝛc.
immer mehr Familien um ihr
zuletztes Haab und an den
Bettelstab, da es nach dem nöthig
gen Wesen nicht gelingt, für
sich und seine Familie Ver-
dienst zu finden.

Ehrfurchtsvollst gehorsamst

Der Koeniglichen Hofbau-Intendanz

unterthänig gehorsamster
Magistrat Garmisch

[signatures]

163

Garmisch, December 30th, 1868

Royal Building Superintendent!

In Humble Presentation by the Magistrates of the Market Town of Garmisch

Re: The Prevalence of Poverty in the Market Town of Garmisch

According to reports heard, the building of a number of large edifices for His Majesty, our beloved King and Lord, is soon to be commenced at Linderhof near Oberammergau.In view of the growing prevalence of poverty and widespread unemployment which have taken on horrifying proportions in the Market Town of Garmisch, we dare to submit to his Royal Building Superintendent the most respectful request, most graciously to condescend that a larger number of the native inhabitants be made of use at the buildings in question and that the native craftsmen, such as cabinetmakers, turners, carvers, bricklayers etc., find a most possible well-disposed consideration.In substantiation of proof for the prevailing poverty here, we take the liberty to call your attention to the fact that when it comes to the payment of taxes, fire insurance or other contributions to public funds, the majority of the inhabitants of the Market Town of Garmisch are not in a position to come up with more than a few pennies, despite the best of intentions to at least partially fulfill their duty towards the state etc. and thus as a result of the proscribed forced collection and the auctioning off of their last goods etc. more and more families are being thrown into abject poverty and a state of beggary whereby even men in the best of years cannot manage to find enough work to feed their families.

In most respectful abeyance
of the Royal Building Superintendent
humbly, the most obedient
Magistrates of Garmisch

Knilling Mayor
Heiligmayr Town Clerk

Above all the itinerary of Ludwig II allows us deep insight into the lifestyle and structure of the King's life. Particularly considering the official diagnosis of the King as mentally disturbed one would expect Ludwig II's itinerary, at least in the last years of his life, to evince signs of confusion, unpredictability, lack of planning, moodiness and flightiness. Nothing of the kind is in the least evident, quite the opposite. To an unprejudiced observer the itinerary reveals, on the contrary, an extraordinarily strongly developed sense of order and desire for structure as well as an unusually strong attitude of steadfastness and consistency bordering on uncompromisingness. Contrary to all expectations, there is also a development over time from more spontaneity in the early years to a firmer, clearer and more transparent order. Even the frequent changing from one place to another, which is often cited in secondary literature and interpreted as a sign of inner disquietude, speaks for the King's stability in that the changes took place in keeping with fixed laws of order and reason. This is especially apparent on hand from the mountain trips. They began in about 1871 during the "steely ride"[2] phase and were obviously undertaken spontaneously without any long-term planning when there were no pressing matters of business at hand. The destination was often only just a mountain hut and they usually lasted two or three days. Later they became part of a strictly adhered to schedule planned long in advance and for years to come. In the early days as well, however, there were a number of reasons for changing places that followed a consistent pattern over many years, for example, the birthdays and name days of Ludwig himself (August 25th) as well as those of the Queen Mother Marie (September 8th and October 15th) and Prince Otto (April 27th and September 30th), which were celebrated for many years at Hohenschwangau. For many years Ludwig II would also honour Richard Wagner's birthday (May 22nd) on Hochkopf. After 1872 the scheduling of the sojourns was subject to an ever stricter time frame with nothing left to chance or the mood of the moment. A suitable period of time was allotted and remained constant over the years for staying at one place, starting with his unloved Residence in Munich down to the last humble, but "valued and precious" mountain hut. After a phase in which different combinations were tested, the mountain trips were organized into appropriate groups based on regional criterion – as anyone who knows the area has to admit – and took place at the same time every year. The only exception to this rule is the year 1881. The time allotted for taking care of government business was also subject to a strict schedule and took place at regular intervals wherever the King happened to be residing at the time, which included his mountain huts. The itinerary provides no points of reference for traits that could indicate mental instability such as chaos, lack of planning, unpredictability and moodiness.

Motive for the Lifestyle

Ludwig II's itinerary also does not offer any evidence that a pathological, unmotivated unsociableness was the main cause for the King's "mountain escapism" or, as Kurt Wilhelm recently expressed it, his supposed cowardly crawling off to the wilderness.[3] Even Hannes Heindl is mistaken here when he assumes that Ludwig II avoided the region around Walchen Lake for a period of time due to an influx of tourists in the area.[4] Ludwig II's itinerary proves on the contrary that the King was not at all bothered about the whole business of the tourists but continued his yearly mountain trips to Hochkopf and Herzogstand as planned long in advance without any curtailments till his death prevented him. For understandable reasons he merely refrained from having these mountain trips "trumpeted about" and spread to all the newspapers. There are perfectly simple and valid explanations for his extended stays in the mountains. His motives are primarily to be seen in connection with overseeing the progress made on the building of his castles or on the completion of the living quarters in them. In the fall of 1870 Schachen became habitable, Castle Linderhof before its completion in 1878, Herrenchiemsee in 1881 and Neuschwanstein in 1884. The circumstance that each of the new castles also had to be allotted a suitable time slot naturally made it necessary to modify the till then valid sojourn schedule. These changes, incidentally, were made for the most part at the cost of time otherwise spent at Schloss Berg and Hohenschwangau and only at the beginning at the cost of time spent

166

at the Residence in Munich. Even if one can't approve of Ludwig's reason for completely striking the Residence from his sojourn schedule in the autumn of 1885 – he was annoyed that his precarious financial situation didn't allow for any of the planned private performances –, one must acknowledge that there was a concrete reason. Even in this case the King's behaviour was not unmotivated. It was not pathological unsociableness but rather a strong sense of affinity with nature which was clearly and unequivocally the primary motive for his sojourns "in the mountains in God's free and sublime nature where I feel at home".[5] The, at that time, well-known publisher and author Georg Hirth characterized the King's bond with nature with the following words: "Not a soul before him, to say nothing of a ruler, has ever achieved such an ideal, well-scheduled and ingenious enhancement of Alpine love".[6]

Aside from his close bond to nature there was another decisive motive for Ludwig II's retreating lifestyle. The King himself speaks of this motive in a letter to Richard Wagner dated January 3rd, 1872: "Yes, you have rightly recognized the deep source of my soul's suffering! It is known that I would not shrink from any sacrifice, no matter how great or painful, if the true well-being of the nation should so demand. Nonetheless, I feel justified in staying in my sphere and not letting myself be pulled down into the vortex of everyday life which repels me even when I must make provisions for it, justified in persevering in my ideal-royal-poetic higher spheres and loneliness like you, my adored friend, unconcerned about the venomous viper's tongues. – With Schiller in the 'Maiden of Orleans' I can say 'Oh, I am not lonely since in solitude I grew to know myself!': Do not regret this but rest assured that my very refusal to compromise myself spiritually with the shallow world has allowed me to preserve the sanctuary of my ideals unharmed, which indirectly perhaps has made it possible for you to complete the great Nibelungen oeuvre. Do not think of this as boasting. The pure fire of exalted enthusiasm cannot be kept alight if the priest concerns himself too much with things of this earth, one cannot serve God and mammon at the same time and this is what is at issue here. –"[7] In this statement Ludwig II makes it very clear that the real reason for his loneliness were his ideals and convictions which the world perceived but did not share. It was not a pathological unsociability that had him

167

choose his lonely lifestyle but the conscious decision to protect and preserve his ideals which he recognized as being righteous. His was not the
loneliness of the fool but the loneliness of one dedicated to upholding
higher ideals.

Bayer. Hauptstaatarchiv: Abt. Kriegsarchiv
(Bavarian State Central Archive: dept. War Archive
Mkr 7856 {Bl 39})

(signature of Ludwig II)

*I am in agreement with the conception as developed here and expect as for the rest,
that Liebert's claims for reimbursement will be taken into all possible consideration
during negotiations with the Finance Ministry.*

Schloss Berg, July 14th, 1870

Ludwig

№ 7550.

Exp. 16/7 70 ...

Kr.M. Exp. 15 Jul. 1870 № 9025.

An

Seine Majestaet

den

KOENIG

vom

Kriegs-Ministerium.

Bitte des Pächters des militärischen ehemaligen evangelischen Gottesackers zu Augsburg Joseph Liebert um käufliche Ueberlassung dieses Pachtobjectes betreffend.

Ich bin mit der hier entwickelten Anschauung einverstanden, erwarte übrigens, daß die Entschädigungsansprüche Lieberts bei den seinerzeitigen Verhandlungen mit dem Finanzministerium nach Thunlichkeit Berücksichtigung finden.

Schloß Berg den 14 Juli 1870.

Ludwig

Euerer Königlichen Majestaet hat der treugehorsamst Unterzeichnete unter Wiedervorlage der mit allerhöchstem Signat vom 25. vorigen Monats zur Berichterstattung herabgeschlossenen Vorstellung des Schreinermeisters Joseph Liebert zu Augsburg vom 21. vorigen Monats allerunterthänigst das Nachstehende zu berichten:

Der allerhöchsten Verordnung vom 11. April 1852 gemäss, die Normen bei der Veräusserung von Staats-Realitäten betreffend, hat dem Vollzuge des Verkaufes einer Staats-Realität eine dem Zwecke entsprechende öffentliche Bekanntmachung vorauszugehen und der Verkauf im Wege der öffentlichen Versteigerung zu bewerkstelligen.

Today at the turn of the 21ˢᵗ century one has to recall to mind the ideas and phenomenon of the times against which Ludwig had to defend his ideals and convictions. Among them were the exaggerated pretensions of high society towards representation, namely, "to personally receive and listen to the twaddle of the more or less odious princely personages",[8] "to exhibit myself to curious gapers and surrender myself as a victim of their ovations",[9] and to function as "decoration at imperial events"[10] or carnival balls. "I hate to the very death this rush to be in a hurry to do nothing as is the case for receptions, balls and festivities of all kinds".[11] Instead of leading a life which "went around in empty, banal circles".[12] King Ludwig II wanted to dedicate himself to the royal task of "living and influencing future generations".[13] The fruit of his oeuvre which he wanted to create, among others, together with Richard Wagner "should be for the benefit and welfare of later generations".[14] As early as 1865 he enthusiastically reassured Richard Wagner: "And after we are both long dead our work will serve as a shining model for posterity, over the centuries it shall enchant and fill hearts with a glowing enthusiasm for art, as divine, as eternal!"[15]

Ludwig II felt his ideal of kingship to be even more threatened by "the contagious poison of modern German-swindle ideas",[16] namely the aspirations of Bismarck's Prussia to establish itself as a great power. Bismarck's politics of blood and iron, allying itself with tempting promises of welfare for both the nation and realm, pursued the goal of raising Germany to heights of unforeseen power and size. Greeted with excited jubilance particularly by the educated middle classes at the time, the movement also enjoyed massive popularity in Bavaria. Enthusiasts demanded that Ludwig II also fall into line and cheer for goals that not only threatened his own political position but that, above all, contradicted his own ideas about the duties of "authentic and true kingship". Ludwig II condemned these strivings because he was convinced that "this Prussian swindle can only lead to trouble!"[17] With astonishing clearness he recognized the essence of this power politics even before it came to the German fratricidal war in 1866. In response to Prince Chlodwig von Hohenlohe-Schillingsfürst's conviction that Prussia was only interested in hegemony over northern Germany, he retorted in April 1866: "For now, but later they will want more."[18] In vain he wished: "That God would protect us from Prussia's claws!"[19] Soon after the war of 1870/71 he was to discover that "the infamous, false", "satanic Prussian politics"[20], in the pursuit of its striving for power, ignored the promises made to him in advance to reward "loyalty with loyalty".[21] "Prussia, for whom Bavaria has performed essential services and helped to achieve some decisive victories, instead of showing its appreciation, treats us as if We, and not poor France, had been its enemies in the last military campaign."[22]

With deep concern Ludwig II also observed the influence of this power politics on the nation's sense of morals. "The trade of war pursued over a longer period of time spoils people's morals, makes them incapable of comprehending large and exulting ideas, apathetic of spiritual enjoyments!"[23] "The currently dominant spirit of the time is horrible, people are perverted, eaten up by the pestilent ideas of modern times, oh, this cannot lead to anything good."[24] When Ludwig II refused to receive the Kaiser-Hero and other representatives of "this insane German kaiser swindle"[25], one must consider what effect such receptions were bound to have had on the "already contaminated populace". Already exposed to propagandistic exploitation by "the agitating trumpeters of the Prussian rulers"[26] and "Bismarck's helpers' helpers"[27], people would necessarily have been given the impression that the King accepted and approved of the Prussian politics. Ludwig II refused to let himself be misused, though, as a front for politics which were in complete opposition to his own principles and convictions. "Without grandiloquence" he declared the following in 1874 to the papal nuncio Bianchi in Munich: "I have enemies, they want me to speak out against the church but I refuse to cooperate, I'm a catholic and sincerely attached to his Holy Father. Tell him that when you write to him."[28] This was Ludwig's picture of a desolate world "with which I was, am, and always will be spiritually at war with and with which I can never be reconciled"[29], a world he wanted to "defy"[30] right from the start.

The King's defiance took shape, not in a vacuum but quite concretely against the universally adored Kaiser-Hero and "head of the military party in Prussia"[31] Crown Prince Friedrich, on the quite memorable occasion of

171

a reception for the equally "crazy" professor and poet Felix Dahn in August of 1873 at Schachen with the following words: "I hate, I despise militarism!"[32] The depth of his despise is apparent in Ludwig's comments about the initiators of the Franco-Prussian War of 1870/71: "Woe to him who precipitated this wretched war in such an irresponsible manner ... the wickedness of violent usurpation, of stealing a crown stained with blood, of gaining a throne by lying and cheating is being demonstrated right now by Napoleon {III}, the criminality of such acts are being revealed in all their naked wretchedness."[33]

In deliberate contrast to the ideology of kaiser as potentate and hero, Ludwig's own political ideal of kingship – ignored till now – was expressed in quite different terms as reported and vouched for by the Master of the Horse Paul von Haufingen: "I would consider it more important to find the right solutions to social questions in my land than if I could become lord of Europe by means of military glory. I would not want to be responsible for the life of one of my citizens in order to serve my selfish purposes. I do not wish from the Creator the fortuna of a conqueror, this madness of princes, but for this happiness, that after my death people will say: Ludwig only strove to be a truly most loyal friend to his people and that he was able to fill his nation with happiness."[34] Against the promises of welfare made by the power ideologists, he declared being able to serve the arts as a "blessing and true happiness for Germany, even for the whole world."[35] This is why he spoke joyfully to Richard Wagner "that this heart will never and cannot stop beating with enthusiasm for all that is noble and exulted, and in keeping with this admonition I, now as a man, respect the dreams of my youth and want, with God's and your help, to breathe life into them".[36] There is no need for exhaustive arguments to prove that such ideas and aspirations would appear to be the useless and unacceptable fantasies of a mentally disturbed person to the power ideologists at the time as well as later.

Ludwig II clearly recognized that clinging to his ideals would force him to live a life in total isolation. This is proved by a statement he made to Richard Wagner: "I believe you imagine (if I may so) that my position is easier than it is. To stand alone, absolutely alone in this comfortless, desolate world, alone with my perceptions, not understood and mistrusted,

Nr. 305 & 306. **Neues Münchener Tagblatt.** Zweites Blatt.

München. Dienstag den 1. und Mittwoch den 2. November 1887. 11. Jahrgang.

Am Sarge König Ludwigs II. in der St. Michaels-Hofkirche zu München.

In der Metropolitan-Pfarrkirche zu Unser Lieben Frau, in der Hofkirche zu St. Kajetan, in der Pfarrkirche zu St. Bonifaz und in der k. Hofkirche zu St. Michael sind die Fürstengrüfte des erlauchten bayerischen Herrscherhauses. Erbaut wurde die Hofkirche zum heil. Michael durch Herzog Wilhelm V. in den Jahren 1583–1591. Die Gruft befindet sich unter dem Presbyterium. Sie bildet ein ge-

räumiges Viereck. In dieses gelangt man durch bequeme breite Stiegen von dem St. Ignatius- und dem Franz Xaverius-Altar aus. Das Gewölbe der Gruft wird durch vier steinerne Säulen getragen. Hierdurch wird die Gruft in ein Mittel- und zwei Seitenschiffe getheilt. Die beiden eisernen Thüren stellen das bayerische Wappen vor. An der Wand im Mittelschiffe steht ein schön vergoldeter Altar

mit dem Bildnisse des gekreuzigten Heilandes. Diesem gegenüber stellt ein Wandgemälde die Auferstehung dar. Vor dem Altar brennt eine Lampe. Rechts vom Altar steht der prächtige Sarg des unvergeßlichen Königs Ludwig II. Die Tage trübe, welche dem Beispiel des Prinz-Regenten und der Prinzen und Prinzessinnen folgen, an Allerseelentag in stiller Andacht in der St. Michael-

On King Ludwig II's coffin in St Michael's Church 1887.
Illustration from "Neues Münchener Tagblatt" from November 1st and 2nd, 1887

that is not a small thing."[37] But for him there was no compromise between the spirit and the non-spirit: "It is not in my nature to be able to compromise. One has to be the way I want one to be. If that is not the case, then one has to do without contact with me."[38] The vacillating judgement of the masses was also not a criteria for him since "I disdain the judgement of the stupid masses".[39] "What does the clear-eyed eagle flying in the air of the sun care about the wretched sparrows screaming after him?"[40] The recipe of those obsessed with success who are always on the lookout to see which way the wind is blowing was not for him either. Rather, he felt duty bound to a higher sense of ethos: "Since the world will not change, so shall we, as you put it so beautifully in your next to the last letter, also not change, but remain steadfast in our loyalty to our ideals."[41] To this purpose he also oriented himself on models whose character impressed him because

173

they held fast to what they recognized to be right "with imperturbable, unwavering loyalty".[42] He accepted that the "slaves of banality" would never be able to comprehend him.[43] This attitude reveals the same inflexible and uncompromising consistency that is manifested in his itinerary. One has to keep this in mind when reading the self-characterization which Ludwig II sent to Richard Wagner in a letter on September 9th, 1876: "You must live for many more long years to come as the glory and greatest pride of the German nation, as the happiness and joy and comfort in this mournful world for your many admirers, above all for your true friends who love you and who are willing to make sacrifices (not just offer cold admiration); for whom loyalty is a high commandment, who never waver, who have no fear of the world as others do; who remain loyal to the dreams of their youth and their true ideals; who in later years do not let their hearts be infected by the deadly poison of oh-so-laudable common sense; among these friends may be counted with all good reasons your loyal, till death parts us, devoted Ludwig".[44] Even at the height of the cabinet funds crisis a few weeks before his death, though, Ludwig's attitude was not so stubborn and unreasonable as to absolutely refuse to consider any of the requested curtailments. On the contrary, a document – obviously surviving only in the form of a copy in the Staatstheaterakt (= State Theatre Act) of Privy Councillor Klug – has recently come to light which proves that Ludwig II, in contradiction to all the self-serving official claims, indeed ordered very drastic economy measures: "To my Court Secretariat. In consideration of prevailing circumstances a reduction in expenditures is called for in all the branches of my court services. It is therefore My Will that the needs of the court staff be limited to the most necessary items and that a drastic simplification of procedures and curtailments of expenditures be implemented. I hereby order My Court Secretariat, in conjunction and with the support of the Head of My Court Staff, to initiate the necessary measures as soon as possible. Hohenschwangau, April 24th, 1886. Ludwig. *Pro copia:* Munich, April 27th, 1886, Royal Court Secretariat. Klug, royal councillor."[45] Nonetheless, Ludwig II justified his past behaviour in his dealings with the "narrow-minded stupidity"[46] of his opponents in a letter dated April 5th/6th 1886 to Prince Ludwig Ferdinand of Bavaria: "People now realize what they had in grandfather (King Ludwig I); when he was still the reigning King, though, they treated him abominably, especially when it came to his art projects, though not just for that reason, till in 1848 they all turned their backs on him."[47]

Concerning[48] Ludwig II's ideals and the overpowering ideologies of his age, history has passed its incorruptible judgement. It has exposed the dream of the power-hungry German strategists, then and later, as the real madness, "this madness of princes to become Lord of Europe by means of military glory", as Ludwig II puts it. Forced through unification and a politics of "blood and iron" into becoming a great power, later a world power, Germany in the end was transformed into a heap of rubble and ruins. On the other hand, history has raised the artistic creations which Ludwig had built in opposition to his *zeitgeist* and held to be absolutely useless and pointless at the time, to the status of landmarks recognized the world over, symbols of a once again prosperous Bavaria. Not least of all due to their incalculable value as a symbol for the deep human desire for a better, more beautiful world free of blood and iron ideologies, they annually attract almost two and half million visitors from all over the world. They guarantee the state a considerable volume of profitable tourist business long after the rash rise and fall of the "terrible German Reich, as, unfortunately, with thanks to the prosaic and cynical Prussianism, shaped by that march Junker."[49] This is why Ludwig II's refusal to succumb to the "contagious pest of the fatal German-swindle"[50] today deserves respect and admiration. It was not motivated by a pathological unsociableness, but by an inflexible steadfastness to hold to his convictions and ideals of kingship "till his last breath".[51] With more right than many ruling "spirits of darkness"[52], then and later, Ludwig II can boast: "Oh, be convinced that We have not fought, struggled, suffered in vain; Parcival remains loyal until death."[53]

An Explanation of the Itinerary

A more detailed version of the itinerary including complete references to the countless documentary proofs for individual days of over 22 reigning years, would have involved a much more extensive volume than this pub-

Abschrift.

Mit Rücksicht auf die bestehenden Verhältnisse ist eine Beschränkung der Ausgaben in allen Zweigen Meines Hofdienstes geboten. Es ist deshalb Mein Wille, daß der Aufwand Meiner Hofstäbe auf das Nothwendige beschränkt und durchgreifende Vereinfachungen und Ersparungen bei denselben herbeigeführt werden.

Ich beauftrage Mein Hofsekretariat, im Benehmen und mit Unterstützung der Chefs Meiner Hofstäbe die hienach erforderlichen Einleitungen alsbald zu treffen.

Hohenschwangau, den 24. April 1886.

(gez.) Ludwig.

An
Mein Hofsekretariat.

Pro copia.
München, den 27. April 1886.
Kgl. Hof-Secretariat.

Klug
d. Rath

lication allowed for. For this reason the itinerary at hand could only be printed in its present highly comprised form. Inevitably this entailed some disadvantages. The citation of documentary proofs for individual days, for the most part archive call numbers, had to necessarily be dispensed with. This generally made it more difficult to check statements and verify important conclusion such as, for example, the working habits of the King. This is the reason for providing an exact description of the source material and the research methods used in order to at least provide a general point of reference for verification.

The layout for the itinerary also proscribed that the data for two full years had to be squeezed onto a single page. It was only possible to achieve this goal for the first years of Ludwig II's reign, 1864 to 1869, by a different treatment the numerous, sometimes several day long "steeling rides" – which, by the way, even by today's standards amounted to athletic performances on an olympic niveau. Though transparency would have dictated naming as many places along the trail of these rides as possible there was not enough room. They were eliminated as separate items on the general schedule and only the starting points of the rides were listed in a separate sequence. The lack of space also didn't allow for including the various reasons for individual trips. On the other hand, this form of layout provided a better overview of the development of King Ludwig II's time management plan.

A certain amount of inaccuracy also exists in this itinerary at the interfaces between place changes. This inaccuracy is due to the fact that the cited signature of the King might have been written early in the morning or, equally possible, late in the evening. This means, for example, that the mountain trip cited in this itinerary as taking place on May 29th and the 30th might possibly have only taken place from late in the evening of the 29th to the early morning of the 30th. It is also possible, though, that Ludwig departed on the trip as early as the evening of the 28th of May and didn't return until sometime on the 31st of May. These types of inaccuracies were only possible to avoid when the exact departure and arrival dates could be found in other sources, for example, in the castle chronicle of Hohenschwangau, letters of the King or from press reports. If departure and arrival occurred on the same day then the destination of the departure date was also noted. Any places or times for which no reliable documentation could be found were marked with a question mark placed immediately behind the questionable data.

Despite all these shortcomings, the substantial interest shown in questions touching on the King Ludwig II's private lifestyle and sojourns would seem to justify publishing the itinerary in its present form since it provides reliable information about many of these questions.

Overview of the Sojourns

1864

March 10th to May 14th: Munich

May 14th to the 26th: Berg, from here riding excursions on

May 17th: around Lake Starnberg

May 18th: around Lake Ammer

May 21st: to Partenkirchen

May 23rd to the 25th: to Weilheim – Peißenberg – Steingaden (May 24th) – Peißenberg – Berg (May 25th)

May 27th to June 18th: Munich

June 19th to July 15th: Bad Kissingen

July 16th to the 30th: Munich

July 30th to August 12th: Bad Schwalbach, from here short trips to:
Darmstadt
Cologne
Frankfurt

August 12th to October 2nd: Hohenschwangau, from here trips and riding excursions on

September 16th to the 17th: Bießenhofen (on horseback) – Munich (by train) – Hohenschwangau

September 29th: Possenhofen

October 2nd: Bießenhofen (on horseback) – Munich (by train)

October 2nd to the 11th: Munich

October 11th to November 30th: Hohenschwangau, from here riding excursions on

October 22nd to the 23rd: Partenkirchen

November 17th: over Fern Pass to Imst

November 22nd to the 23rd: Innsbruck

November 30th: Steingaden – Weilheim – Munich

December 1st to the 30th: Munich

1865

January 1st to May 17th: Munich

May 17th to July 29th: Berg, from here riding excursions on

May 22nd: Feldafing (via Seeshaupt)

May 23rd to the 24th: Hohenschwangau – Partkirchen (overnight?) – Krün? – Vorderriß? – Achen Pass? – Tegernsee – Berg (arrival on May 25th at 2:00 a.m.)

May 30th to the 31st: among others, Schliersee with a visit to the inn "Fischerliesl" on May 31st

June 5th to the 8th: Wofratshausen – Benediktbeuern – Walchensee – Vorderriß – Partenkirchen – Hohenschwangau (June 8th at 4:00 p.m.) – Berg

June 12th to the 13th: Schlehdorf (overnight there)

June 19th to the 22nd: Steingaden – Hohenschwangau – Reutte – Linderhof – Brunnenkopf – Berg

June 27th to the 30th: Pürschling? – Linderhof[54]

July 3rd to the 8th: Hochkopf – Grammersberg

July 17th to the 23rd: Vorderriß – Hochkopf

July 29th: Hohenschwangau (on horseback)

July 19th to October 1st: Hohenschwangau, from here riding excursions on

August 2nd to the 8th: Brunnenkopf – Pürschling – Halbammer

September 11th to the 18th: Tegelberg – Kenzen – Linderhof

October 1st: Bießenhofen (on horseback) – Munich (by train)

October 1st to the 3rd: Munich

October 4th to the 5th: Horseback ride from Berg? to Steingaden (overnight?) and Hohenschwangau

October 5th to the 17th: Hohenschwangau

October 17th to the 19th: Munich

October 19th to November 2nd: via Tölz – Vorderriß, (continuing on horseback?) Partenkirchen – Allgäu to Switzerland

November 2nd to December 4th: Hohenschwangau

December 4th to the 5th: Horseback ride to Partenkirchen (overnight) – Benediktbeuern – Tölz – Holzkirchen and further on by train to Munich

December 5th to the 31st: Munich

1866

January 1st to May 11th: Munich
May 11th to June 18th: Berg, from here on
May 21st to the 24th: Horseback ride to Bießen-
hofen to continue on to Triebschen in
Switzerland
June 19th to the 30th: Munich, from here trips
on
  July 25th to the 27th: Bamberg
June 30th to July 12th: Berg and Rosen Island
July 12th to August 4th: Munich
August 4th to September 29th: Berg, from here
trips and mountain excursions on
August 7th to the 9th: Brunnenkopf[55]
August 23rd to the 28th: Horseback trip to Lin-
derhof (August 23rd) – Partenkirchen-
Hochkopf (August 24th to the 25th) – Her-
zogstand (August 26th) – Ettal – Linder-
hof – Plansee – Reutte – Steingaden
(August 27th) – Berg (August 28th)
September 2nd to the 7th: Tegelberg (horseback
trip)
September 15th to the 17th: Vorderriß
September 29th to October 2nd: to Peißenberg
(by train) continuing on to Hohenschwan-
gau (on horseback). From there on horse-
back on October 1st to Steingaden and on
October 2nd to Munich
October 2nd to the 12th: Munich
October 13th to the 14th: Berg
October 14th to November 9th: Hohenschwan-
gau, from here horseback trips on
November 3rd to the 5th: Innsbruck
(November 3rd) – Partenkirchen (November
4th) – Hohenschwangau (November 5th)
November 8th to the 9th: Horseback ride to
Steingaden (November 8th) – Weilheim –
Munich (November 9th)
November 10th to December 12th: Trip through
Franconia:
Bayreuth – Hof – Bamberg – Bad Kissin-
gen – Aschaffenburg – Würzburg – Nürn-
berg
December 13th to the 21st: Hohenschwangau
December 21st to the 31st: Munich

1867

January 1st to May 11th: Munich
May 11th to June 26th: Berg, from here trips and
horseback excursions on
May 17th to the 19th: Mountain excursion:
Horseback ride over Reutte? and
Garmisch? back to Berg
May 25th to the 28th: Schliersee with detours to
Bayrischzell and Landl on May 25th. On
May 26th through Kaiserklause to Vorderriß
May 31st to June 2nd: Eisenach
June 4th to the 6th: Horseback ride to Achen
Lake and to Fügen in the Ziller Valley, con-
tinuing on by post coach to Mayrhofen and
by foot to Finkenberg and Teufelssteg
June 12th to the 14th: Mountain excursion: Lin-
derhof?
June 21st to the 23rd: Hochkopf
June 27th to the 30th: Munich
July 1st to the 20th: Berg, from here mountain
excursions on
July 12th to the 16th: Herzogstand
July 21st to the 29th: Paris
July 30th: Munich
July 30th to August 23rd: Berg, from here trips
and mountain excursions on
August 1st to the 2nd: Linderhof
August 7th to the 10th: Sojern (and Grammers-
berg?)
August 15th to the 18th: Hohenschwangau
(August 15th/16th) – Augsburg (August 17th)
– Prien/Chiem Lake (August 18th)
August 23rd to the 24th: Horseback ride over
Pürschling and Brunnenkopf to Hohen-
schwangau
August 24th to September 16th: Hohenschwan-
gau
September 16th to the 30th: Berg
September 30th to October 29th: Hohenschwan-
gau, from here trip on
October 6th: Augsburg
October 29th to November 7th: Munich
November 7th to December 20th: Hohenschwan-
gau
December 20th to the 21st: Partenkirchen
December 21st to the 31st: Munich

1868

January 1st to May 11th: Munich
May 11th to July 10th: Berg, from here trips and
mountain excursions on
May 25th to the 29th: Hochkopf (May 25th) –
Berg (May 26th) – Partenkirchen – Hohen-
schwangau (May 27th/28th) – Steingaden
(May 28th) – Berg (May 29th)
June 4th to the 8th: Brunnenkopf – Hohen-
schwangau (from here on June 6th 8:00 p.m.
to June 8th) – Berg
June 11th: Munich
June 16th to the 18th: Herzogstand – Hohen-
schwangau – Berg
June 21st: Munich
June 30th to July 4th: Kenzen – Hohenschwan-
gau – Berg
July 8th: Vorderriß?
July 11th to the 22nd: Hohenschwangau
July 22nd to August 2nd: Berg, from here trips
and mountain excursions on
July 26th to the 28th: Linderhof – Reutte –
Hohenschwangau – Berg
July 30th: Munich
August 2nd to the 10th: Bad Kissingen
August 11th to October 14th: Berg, from here
trips and mountain excursions on
August 18th to the 24th: Sojern – Vorderriß –
(and Grammersberg?)
August 24th to the 27th: Hohenschwangau
September 4th to the 6th: Mountain excursion:
Linderhof?
September 8th to the 10th: Hohenschwangau
September 17th to the 20th: Eschenlohe – Linder-
hof – Brunnenkopf
September 24th to the 25th: Mountain excursion
September 30th to October 2nd: Hohenschwan-
gau
October 12th to the 14th: Munich
October 14th to 28th:
October 14th to the 18th: Hohenschwangau
October 18th to 22nd: Linderhof
October 22nd: Berg
October 23rd to the 25th: Munich
October 25th to the 28th: Berg
October 29th to December 31st:
October 29th to November 7th: Linderhof
November 7th to the 13th: Hohenschwangau

November 13th to the 16th: Munich
November 16th to December 9th: Hohen-
schwangau
December 9th to the 10th: Linderhof
December 12th to the 21st: Hohenschwangau
December 21st to the 22nd: Partenkirchen
December 22nd to the 31st: Munich

1869

January 1st to May 11th: Munich
May 11th to June 13th: Berg, from her mountain
excursions on
May the 24th?: Grammersberg?
May 28th to the 30th: Herzogstand?
June 4th to the 8th: Mountain excursion, with
stays on June 6th/7th at Linderhof
June 13th to the 27th: Hohenschwangau, from
here trips and mountain excursions on
June 16th to the 18th: Tegelberg Hut
June 18th to the 22nd: Berg and Munich
June 22nd to the 24th: Kenzen Hut
June 27th to July 16th: Berg, from here moun-
tain excursions on
July 2nd to the 4th: Vorderriß (and Herzog-
stand?)
July 8th to the 11th: Grammersberg – Sojern
July 16th to August 4th: Hohenschwangau
August 4th to the 15th: Linderhof (also Brun-
nenkopf?, Pürschling?)
August 15th to the 27th:
August 15th to the 18th: Berg
August 18th to the 20th: Munich
August 21st to the 22nd: Landshut
August 23rd to the 24th: Berg
August 24th to the 27th: Hohenschwangau
August 27th to October 14th: Berg, from here
trips and mountain excursions on
August 31st to September 3rd: Hochkopf
September 7th to the 10th: Hohenschwangau
September 10th: Berg
September 10th to the 11th: Schweinfurt
September 15th to the 17th: Sojern and
Schöttelkarspitze
September 23rd to the 24th: Schlehdorf
September 29th to October 2nd: Hohen-
schwangau
October 7th to the 9th: Halbammer Hut

181

October 14th to the 29th:
    October 14th to the 17th: Hohenschwangau
    October 17th to the 18th: Herzogstand
    October 20th: Berg
    October 21st to the 22nd: Linderhof
    October 23rd to the 29th: Munich
October 29th to December 31st:
    October 30th to the 31st: Partenkirchen
    November 1st to the 2nd?: Vorderriß
    November 3rd? to the 9th: Linderhof
    November 9th to December 23rd: Hohenschwangau
    December 24th to the 27th: Munich
    December 27th to the 31st: Hohenschwangau

1870

January 1st to May 10th:
    January 1st to April 26th: Munich
    April 26th to the 29th: Hohenschwangau
    April 29th to May 10th: Munich
May 11th to the 22nd: Berg
May 23rd to the 26th: Linderhof (+ Vorderriß?)
May 27th to June 4th: Berg
June 5th to the 10th: Hochkopf – Grammersberg – Vorderriß
June 11th to the 17th: Berg
June 18th to July 14th:
    June 18th to the 20th: Kenzen
    June 20th to July 11th: Hohenschwangau
    July 11th to the 14th (noon): Linderhof – Brunnenkopf – Linderhof
July 14th to the 16th: Schloss Berg (from the evening of July 14th)
July 17th to the 30th: Munich
July 31st to August 24th: Berg
August 25th to September 7th:
    August 25th to the 26th: Hohenschwangau
    August 27th to September 7th: Berg
September 8th to October 5th:
    September 8th to the 10th: Hohenschwangau
    September 10th to October 5th: Berg
October 6th to the 9th:
    October 6th: Herzogstand
October 7th to the 9th: Schachen (first sojourn!)
October 9th to the 14th: Berg and Munich
October 14th to the 26th:
    October 14th to the 17th: Hohenschwangau

October 17th to the 22nd: Linderhof
October 23rd? to the 26th: Partenkirchen
October 27th to November 4th: Munich
November 4th to December 31st:
    November 4th to the 5th: Linderhof
    November 5th to December 12th: Hohenschwangau
    December 13th to the 15th: Linderhof
    December 16th to the 24th: Hohenschwangau
    December 24th to the 28th: Munich
    December 28th to the 31st: Hohenschwangau

1871

January 1st to the 15th:
    January 1st to the 4th: Linderhof
    January 4th to the 15th: Hohenschwangau
January 15th to May 11th:
January 15th to the 16th: Partenkirchen
January 16th to April 27th: Munich
April 27th to May 2nd: Hohenschwangau
May 2nd to the 11th: Munich
May 11th to the 20th: Berg
May 21st to the 27th: (Vorderriß? +) – Linderhof – Hochkopf
May 28th to June 12th:
    May 28th to June 3rd: Berg
    June 4th to the 5th: Mountain excursion?
    June 6th to the 12th: Berg
June 13th to July 11th:
    June 13th to the 18th: Linderhof (+ Pürschling? or Halbammer?)
    June 18th to the 22nd: Hohenschwangau
    June 22nd to the 25th: Tegelberg
    June 25th to July 9th: Hohenschwangau
    July 9th to the 11th: Brunnenkopf
July 12th to August 21st:
    July 12th to the 24th: Berg
    July 25th to the 26th: Grammersberg
    July 27th to the 31st: Berg
    August 1st to the 5th: Sojern – Krün – Schachen
    August 6th to the 15th: Berg, on August 10th also in Schwandorf and Regensburg
    August 16th to the 17th?: Herzogstand?
    August 18th to the 21st: Berg

182

August 22nd to the 29th:
    August 22nd to the 24th: Linderhof
    August 24th to the 27th: Hohenschwangau
    August 27th to the 29th: Linderhof
August 30th to September 7th: Berg
September 7th to the 13th:
    September 7th to the 10th: Hohenschwangau
    September 10th to the 13th: Linderhof
September 14th to the 21st: Berg
September 22nd to the 27th: Linderhof
September 27th to October 14th:
    September 27th to the 29th: Berg
    September 29th to October 2nd: Hohenschwangau
    October 2nd to the 4th: Berg
    October 5th to the 8th: Schachen
    October 8th to the 14th: Berg and Munich
October 14th to the 27th:
    October 14th to the 17th: Hohenschwangau
    October 17th to the 21st: Linderhof
    October 22nd to the 24th: Partenkirchen
    October 25th? to the 27th: Vorderriß
October 27th to November 5th: Munich
November 6th to December 31st:
    November 5th to the 6th: Berg
    November 6th to the 7th: Linderhof
    November 8th to the 18th: Hohenschwangau
    November 18th to the 20th: Linderhof
    November 21st to December 24th: Hohenschwangau
    December 25th to the 30th: Munich
    December 30th to the 31st: Hohenschwangau

1872

January 1st to the 16th:
    January 1st to the 4th: Linderhof
    January 4th to the 16th: Hohenschwangau
January 16th to May 11th:
    January 16th to the 17th: Partenkirchen, then Munich
May 11th to the 31st:
    May 11th to the 13th: Berg
    May 14th to the 22nd: Vorderriß – Hochkopf – Altlach – Herzogstand
    May 23rd to the 31st: Berg
June 1st to the 9th: Linderhof – Pürschling – Brunnenkopf

June 10th to the 14th: Berg
June 15th to July 20th:
    June 15th to the 20th: (Kenzen? and) Tegelberg
    June 20th to July 20th: Hohenschwangau
July 21st to August 7th:
    July 21st to the 25th: Berg
    July 26th to the 28th: Grammersberg
    July 29th to the 31st: Berg
    August 1st to the 2nd: Munich
    August 3rd to the 7th: Berg
    August 8th to the 10th: Sojern – Krün
    August 11th to the 15th: Schachen
    August 16th to the 17th: Linderhof
August 18th to the September 7th:
    August 18th to the 26th: Berg
    August 27th to the 28th: Halbammer
    August 29th to September 7th: Berg
September 7th to the 13th:
    September 7th to the 10th: Hohenschwangau
    September 11th to the 13th: Linderhof – Hochkopf
September 14th to October 3rd: Berg
October 4th to the 10th: Schachen
October 10th to the 14th:
    October 10th to the 12th: Berg
    October 13th to the 14th: Munich
October 15th to the 28th:
    October 15th to the 17th: Hohenschwangau
    October 17th to the 23rd?: Linderhof
    October 24th to the 25th: Partenkirchen
    October 26th to the 28th: Vorderriß
October 28th to November 5th: Munich
November 6th to December 31st:
    November 6th to the 9th: Schachen
    November 9th to the 17th: Hohenschwangau
    November 18th to the 20th: Linderhof
    November 21st to December 23rd: Hohenschwangau
    December 23rd to the 28th: Munich
    December 28th to the 31st: Hohenschwangau

1873

January 1st to the 19th:
    January 1st to the 4th: Linderhof
    January 4th to the 19th: Hohenschwangau

- January 19th to May 11th:
  - January 19th to the 20th: Partenkirchen
  - January 20th to February 23rd: Munich
  - February 23rd to the 26th: Hohenschwangau
  - February 27th to May 11th: Munich
- May 11th to the 19th: Berg
- May 20th to June 1st:
  - May 20th to the 24th: Vorderriß – Hochkopf
  - May 25th to June 1st: Berg
- June 2nd to the 8th: Brunnenkopf (– Pürschling) – Linderhof (June 6th to the 8th)
- June 9th to the 17th: Berg
- June 18th to the 22nd:
  - June 18th to the 19th: Herzogstand
  - June 20th to the 21st: Grammersberg
  - June 22nd: Vorderriß
- June 23rd to the 28th: Berg
- June 29th to August 3rd:
  - June 29th to July 1st: Kenzen
  - July 1st to the 31st: Hohenschwangau
  - July 31st to August 3rd: Tegelberg
- August 3rd to the 11th:
  - August 3rd to the 6th: Linderhof
  - August 7th to the 11th: Berg
- August 12th to the 21st: Sojern?– Krün (August 14th) – Schachen
- August 22nd to September 7th:
  - August 22nd to the 24th: Berg
  - August 24th to the 27th: Hohenschwangau
  - August 28th to the 29th: Linderhof
  - August 30th to the 31st: Pürschling
  - September 1st to the 2nd: Halbammer
  - September 2nd: Unterammergau
  - September 3rd to the 7th: Berg
- September 7th to the 16th:
  - September 7th to 10th: Hohenschwangau
  - September 11th to the 14th: Linderhof
  - September 15th to the 16th: Hochkopf – Altlach
- September 17th to the 29th: Berg
- September 29th to October 8th:
  - September 29th to October 1st: Hohenschwangau
  - October 1st to the 3rd: Linderhof
  - October 4th to the 8th: Schachen
- October 9th the 14th: Berg
- October 14th to the 29th:
  - October 14th to the 17th: Hohenschwangau
  - October 17th to the 23rd: Linderhof
  - October 24th to the 26th?: Partenkirchen
  - October 27th to the 29th: Vorderriß
- October 29th to November 9th: Munich
- November 9th to December 31st:
  - November 9th to the 11th: Linderhof
  - November 11th to the 22nd: Hohenschwangau
  - November 23rd to the 24th: Linderhof
  - November 24th to December 13th: Hohenschwangau
  - December 14th to the 16th: Linderhof?
  - December 17th to the 31st: Hohenschwangau

1874

- January 1st to February the 11th:
  - January 1st to the 4th: Linderhof
  - January 5th to the 28th: Hohenschwangau
  - January 29th to the 31st: Linderhof
  - February 1st to the 11th: Hohenschwangau
- February 11th to May 11th:
  - February 11th to the 12th: Partenkirchen
  - February 14th to April 26th: Munich
  - April 26th to the 29th: Hohenschwangau
  - April 30th to May 11th: Munich
- May 11th to the 19th: Berg
- May 19th to the 25th: Vorderriß – Hochkopf – Linderhof
- May 26th to June 5th: Berg
- June 6th to the 14th: (Herzogstand?) – Linderhof – Brunnenkopf
- June 15th to the 20th: Berg
- June 21st to the 26th: Pürschling – Vorderriß – (Grammersberg?)
- June 27th to July 4th: Berg
- July 5th to August 7th:
  - July 5th to the 7th: Kenzen
  - July 7th to August 4th: Hohenschwangau
  - August 4th to the 7th: Tegelberg
- August 7th to the 20th:
  - August 7th to the 12th: Linderhof – Halbammer
  - August 13th to the 20th: Berg
- August 21st to the 28th: Paris, Versailles
- August 29th to the September 7th: Berg
- September 7th to the 15th?:
  - September 7th to 10th: Hohenschwangau
  - September 10th to the 15th?: Linderhof

September 16th? to the 23rd:
September 16th? to the 20th: Schachen
September 21st to the 23rd: Sojern
September 24th to October 14th:
September 24th to the 29th: Berg
September 29th to October 2nd: Hohen-
schwangau
October 2nd to the 8th: Berg
October 8th to the 11th: Schachen
October 12th to the 14th: Berg
October 14th to the 29th:
October 14th to the 17th: Hohenschwangau
October 17th to the 22nd: Linderhof
October 23rd to the 26th: Partenkirchen
October 27th to the 29th: Vorderriß
October 29th to November 13th: Munich
November 13th to December 31st:
November 13th to the 14th: Linderhof
November 14th to December 5th: Hohen-
schwangau
December 5th to the 9th: Linderhof?
December 9th to the 22nd: Hohenschwangau
December 23rd to the 29th: Munich
December 29th to the 31st: Hohen-
schwangau

1875

January 1st to the 24th:
January 1st to the 4th: Linderhof
January 4th to the 24th: Hohenschwangau
January 24th to May 11th:
January 24th to the 25th: Partenkirchen
January 25th to April 30th: Munich
April 30th to May 2nd: Herrenchiemsee
May 3rd to the 11th: Munich
May 11th to the 19th: Berg
May 19th to the 24th: Vorderriß – Hochkopf
May 25th to June 5th:
May 25th to the 29th: Linderhof
May 30th to June 5th: Berg
June 6th to the 15th: Brunnenkopf -- Pürsch-
ling – Linderhof – Halbammer
June 16th to the 26th: Berg
June 27th to July 5th: Herzogstand –Sojern –
Vorderriß – Grammersberg
July 6th to the 9th: Berg
July 10th to August 8th:
July 10th to the 12th: Kenzen

July 12th to August 5th: Hohenschwangau
August 5th to the 8th: Tegelberg
August 8th to the 13th: Linderhof
August 14th to the 23rd: Berg and Munich
(August 22nd)
August 24th to the 27th: Reims
August 28th to the September 4th: Berg
September 5th to the 19th:
September 5th to 7th: Linderhof
September 8th to the 10th: Hohenschwangau
September 10th to the 19th: Linderhof
September 19th to the 23rd: Schachen
September 24th to October 14th: Berg (October
8th to the 10th unclear, probably mountain
excursion)
October 14th to the 30th:
October 14th to the 17th: Hohenschwangau
October 17th to the 23rd: Linderhof
October 24th to 26th?: Partenkirchen
October 27th? to the 30th: Vorderriß
October 30th to November 12th: Munich
November 12th to December 31st:
November 12th to the 13th: Linderhof
November 14th to December 5th: Hohen-
schwangau
December 5th to the 10th: Linderhof
December 10th to the 22nd: Hohen-
schwangau
December 22nd to the 28th: Munich
December 28th to the 31st: Hohen-
schwangau

1876

January 1st to the 28th:
January 1st to the 4th: Linderhof
January 4th to the 28th: Hohenschwangau
January 28th to May 11th:
January 28th to the 29th: Partenkirchen
January 29th to February 26th: Munich
February 26th to March 4th: Hohen-
schwangau
March 4th to the 7th: Linderhof
March 7th to May 11th: Munich
May 11th to the 19th: Berg
May 19th to the 24th: Vorderriß – Hochkopf
May 25th to June 6th:
May 25th? to the 30th: Linderhof
May 31st to June 6th: Berg

June 7th to the 16th: Brunnenkopf – Pürschling – Linderhof – (Halbammer?)
June 17th to the 23rd: Berg
June 24th to July 2nd: Herzogstand –Sojern – Vorderriß – (Grammersberg?)
July 3rd to the 9th: Berg
July 10th to August 16th:
    July 10th to the 12th:Kenzen
    July 12th to August 4th: Hohenschwangau
    August 4th to the 5th: Berg
    August 6th to the 9th: Bayreuth
    August 10th to the 13th: Hohenschwangau
    August 13th to the 16th: Tegelberg
August 17th to the 30th:
    August 16th to the 19th?: Linderhof
    August 19th? to the 25th: Schachen
    August 25th to the 26th: Berg
    August 26th to the 30th: Bayreuth
August 31st to September 9th: Berg
September 9th to the 16th: Linderhof
September 17th to the 25th:
    September 17th to the 18th: Hochkopf
    September 19th to the 25th: Schachen
September 25th to October 14th: Berg
October 14th to the 30th:
    October 14th to the 17th: Hohenschwangau
    October 17th to the 23rd: Linderhof
    October 24th to 27th: Partenkirchen
    October 28th to the 30th: Vorderriß
October 31st to November 10th: Munich
November 10th to December 31st:
    November 10th to the 12th: Linderhof
    November 12th to December 10th: Hohenschwangau
    December 10th to the 15th: Linderhof
    December 15th to the 22nd: Hohenschwangau
    December 22nd to the 28th: Munich
    December 28th to the 31st: Hohenschwangau

1877

January 1st to the 30th:
    January 1st to the 4th: Linderhof
    January 4th to the 30th: Hohenschwangau
January 30th to May 11th:
    January 30th to the 31st: Partenkirchen
    January 31st to February 11th: Munich

February 11th to the 13th: Hohenschwangau
February 13th to the 14th: Linderhof
February 15th to April 3rd: Munich
April 3rd to the 9th: Hohenschwangau
April 9th to May 11th: Munich
May 11th to the 20th: Berg
May 21st to the 24th: Vorderriß – Hochkopf
May 24th to June 9th:
    May 24th: Unternogg
    May 25th? to June 1st: Linderhof
    June 1st to the 9th: Berg
June 10th to the 17th: Herzogstand? – Sojern? – Vorderriß – Grammersberg?
June 18th to the 25th: Berg
June 26th to the July 3rd: – Pürschling? – Brunnenkopf – Linderhof – Halbammer
July 4th to the 11th: Berg
July 11th to August 10th:
    July 11th to the 14th: Kenzen
    July 14th to August 7th: Hohenschwangau
    August 7th to the 10th: Tegelberg
August 10th to the 16th: Linderhof
August 17th to the 20th: Berg
August 21st to the 26th: Schachen
August 27th to the 31st: Berg
September 1st to the 9th: Linderhof
September 10th to the 17th: Berg
September 18th to the 26th: Schachen
September 27th to the 30th: Berg
October 1st to the 6th: Linderhof
October 6th to the 14th: Berg
October 15th to the 30th:
    October 15th to the 17th: Hohenschwangau
    October 17th to the 24th: Linderhof
    October 24th to 26th?: Partenkirchen
    October 27th? to the 30th: Vorderriß
October 30th to November 11th: Munich
November 11th to December 31st:
    November 11th to the 16th: Linderhof
    November 16th to December 13th: Hohenschwangau
    December 13th to the 18th: Linderhof
    December 18th to the 25th: Hohenschwangau
    December 25th to the 29th: Munich
    December 30th to the 31st: Hohenschwangau

1878

January 1st to February 10th:
  January 1st to the 4th: Linderhof
  January 4th to the 21st?: Hohenschwangau
  January 22nd to the 29th: Linderhof
  January 29th to February 10th: Hohenschwangau
February 10th to May 11th:
  February 10th to the 11th: Partenkirchen
  February 11th to March 18th: Munich
  March 19th: Berg – Linderhof
  March 20th to the 28th: Munich
  March 29th: Linderhof
  March 30th to April 4th: Munich
  April 4th to the 17th: Hohenschwangau
  April 17th to May 11th: Munich
May 11th to the 19th: Berg
May 20th to the 24th: Vorderriß – Hochkopf
May 25th? to June 3rd: Linderhof
June 4th? to the 12th: Halbammer? – Pürschling – Linderhof – Brunnenkopf
June 13th to the 22nd: Berg
June 23rd to July 4th: Herzogstand –Sojern – Grammersberg?
July 5th to the 9th: Berg
July 10th to August 10th:
  July 10th to the 12th: Kenzen
  July 13th to August 7th: Hohenschwangau
  August 7th to the 10th: Tegelberg
August 11th to the 18th: Linderhof
August 19th to the 23rd: Berg
August 23rd September 1st:
  August 23rd to the 25th: Hochkopf
  August 26th to September 1st: Schachen
September 2nd to the 14th: Berg
September 15th to the 21st: Linderhof
September 22nd? to the 30th: Schachen
October 1st to the 14th: Berg
October 15th to the 30th:
  October 15th to the 26th?: Linderhof
  October 27th? to the 30th: Vorderriß
October 31st to November 11th: Munich
November 11th to December 31st:
  November 11th to the 13th: Linderhof
  November 13th to December 4th: Hohenschwangau
  December 4th to the 12th: Linderhof
  December 12th to the 31st: Hohenschwangau

1879

January 1st to February 10th:
  January 1st to the 5th: Linderhof
  January 5th to the 22nd: Hohenschwangau
  January 22nd to the 31st: Linderhof
  January 31st to February 10th: Hohenschwangau
February 10th to May 11th:
  February 10th to the 11th: Partenkirchen
  February 11th to April 5th: Munich
  April 6th to the 19th: Hohenschwangau
  April 20th to May 11th: Munich
May 11th to the 19th: Berg
May 19th to the 24th: Vorderriß – Hochkopf
May 24th to June 3rd: Linderhof
June 4th to the 11th: – Brunnenkopf – Pürschling – Halbammer
June 12th to the 21st: Berg
June 22nd to the 29th: Herzogstand –Sojern – Grammersberg?
June 30th to July 9th: Berg
July 10th to August 11th:
  July 10th to the 12th: Kenzen
  July 13th to August 8th: Hohenschwangau
  August 8th to the 11th: Tegelberg
August 12th to the 22nd?: Linderhof
August 23rd to the 30th: Schachen
August 31st to September 10th: Berg
September 11th to the 20th: Linderhof
September 21st to the 30th : Schachen
October 1st to the 14th: Berg
October 15th to the 30th:
  October 15th? to the 26th: Linderhof
  October 27th? to the 30th: Vorderriß
October 31st to November 14th: Munich
November 14th to December 31st:
  November 14th to the 15th: Linderhof
  November 16th to December 11th: Hohenschwangau
  December 11th to the 19th: Linderhof
  December 19th to the 31st: Hohenschwangau

1880

January 1st to February 10th:
  January 1st to the 5th: Linderhof
  January 5th to the 22nd: Hohenschwangau
  January 22nd to the 31st: Linderhof

187

January 31st to February 10th: Hohen-
schwangau
February 10th to May 11th:
 February 10th to the 11th: Partenkirchen
 February 11th to April 6th: Munich
 April 6th to the 19th: Hohenschwangau
 April 19th to May 11th: Munich
May 11th to the 19th: Berg
May 19th to the 24th: Vorderriß – Hochkopf
May 25th? to June 3rd: Linderhof
June 4th to the 12th: – Brunnenkopf –
 Pürschling – Halbammer?
June 12th to the 21st: Berg
June 22nd to the 30th: Herzogstand –Sojern –
 Grammersberg
July 1st to the 9th: Berg
July 10th to August 10th:
 July 10th to the 12th: Kenzen
 July 12th to August 7th: Hohenschwangau
 August 7th to the 10th: Tegelberg
August 10th to the 21st: Linderhof
August 21st to the 29th: Schachen
August 29th to September 7th: Berg
September 8th to the 18th: Linderhof
September 18th to the 30th: Schachen
September 30th to October 14th: Berg
October 15th to the 31st:
 October 15th to the 26th: Linderhof
 October 26th to the 31st: Vorderriß
October 31st to November 13th: Munich
November 13th to December 31st:
 November 13th to the 14th: Linderhof
 November 14th to December 19th: Hohen-
 schwangau
 December 19th to the 23rd: Linderhof
 December 23rd to the 31st: Hohenschwan-
 gau

1881

January 1st to February 10th:
 January 1st to the 5th: Linderhof
 January 5th to the 22nd: Hohenschwangau
 January 22nd to the 31st: Linderhof
 February 1st to the 10th: Hohenschwangau
February 10th to May 11th:
 February 10th to the 12th: Partenkirchen
 February 12th to April 7th: Munich
 April 7th to the 22nd: Hohenschwangau
 April 23rd to May 11th: Munich

May 11th to the 19th: Berg
May 19th to the 24th: Vorderriß – Hochkopf
May 25th to June 11th: Linderhof
June 12th to the 15th: Halbammer Hut
June 15th to the 27th: Berg
June 27th to July 15th: Switzerland
July 15th to the 17th: Berg
July 18th to August 15th:
 July 18th to the 20th: Kenzen
 July 20th to August 13th: Hohenschwangau
 August 13th to the 15th: Tegelberg
August 15th to the 23rd: Linderhof
August 24th to the 31st: Schachen
September 1st to the 14th:
 September 1st to the 4th: Berg
 September 5th to the 11th: Herzogstand –
 Sojern – Vorderriß – Grammersberg
 September 11th to the 14th: Berg
September 15th to the 19th: Linderhof
September 20th to the 27th: Schachen
September 28th to October 7th:
 September 28th: Berg
 September 29th to October 7th: Herren-
 chiemsee (first longer sojourn)
October 7th to the 14th: Berg
October 15th to the 30th:
 October 15th to the 17th?: Linderhof
 October 17th? to the 18th: Pürschling
 October 19th? to the 21st: Brunnenkopf
 October 21st to the 26th?: Linderhof
 October 27th? to the 30th: Vorderriß
October 31st to November 13th: Munich
November 13th to December 31st:
 November 13th to the 15th: Linderhof
 November 15th to December 10th: Hohen-
 schwangau
 December 10th to the 19th: Linderhof
 December 19th to the 31st: Hohen-
 schwangau

1882

January 1st to February 10th:
 January 1st to the 5th: Linderhof
 January 5th to the 22nd: Hohenschwangau
 January 22nd to the 31st: Linderhof
 February 1st to the 10th: Hohenschwangau
February 10th to May 11th:
 February 10th to the 11th: Partenkirchen
 February 12th to April 8th: Munich

April 9th to the 23rd: Hohenschwangau
April 24th to May 11th: Munich
May 11th to the 14th: Berg
May 14th to the 18th: Vorderriß – Hochkopf
May 18th to the 22nd: Linderhof
May 22nd to June 17th: Hohenschwangau
June 17th to the 25th: Linderhof
June 26th to July 4th:
    June 26th to the 28th: Brunnenkopf
    June 29th to July 1st: Pürschling
    July 2nd to the 4th: Halbammer
July 5th? to the 9th: Berg
July 11th to the 19th:
    July 11th? to the 13th?: Herzogstand?
    July 14th to the 16th: Sojern
    July 17th to the 19th: Grammersberg
July 20th to August 21st:
    July 20th to the 21st: Berg
    July 22nd to the 24th: Kenzen
    July 24th to August 18th: Hohenschwangau
    August 18th to the 21st: Tegelberg
August 22nd to September 1st:
    August 22nd to the 23rd: Linderhof
    August 24th to September 1st: Schachen
September 2nd to the 8th: Berg
September 9th to the 19th: Linderhof
September 20th? to the 27th: Schachen
September 28th to October 7th:
    September 28th: Berg
    eptember 29th to October 7th: Herren-
    chiemsee
October 8th to the 14th: Berg
October 15th to the 30th:
    October 15th to the 26th: Linderhof
    October 27th to the 30th: Vorderriß
October 31st to November 13th: Munich
November 13th to December 31st:
    November 13th to the 22nd: Linderhof
    November 22nd to December 19th: Hohen-
    schwangau
    December 19th to the 23rd: Fernstein – Lin-
    derhof
    December 24th to the 31st: Hohen-
    schwangau

1883

January 1st to February 10th:
    January 1st to the 5th: Linderhof
    January 6th to the 22nd: Hohenschwangau

January 23rd to the 31st: Linderhof
February 1st to the 10th: Hohenschwangau
February 11th to May 11th:
    February 11th to the 12th: Partenkirchen
    February 12th to April 9th: Munich
    April 9th to the 23rd: Hohenschwangau
    April 24th to May 11th: Munich
May 12th to the 14th: Berg
May 15th to the 18th: Vorderriß – Hochkopf
May 19th to the 23rd: Linderhof
May 23rd to June 16th: Hohenschwangau
June 16th to the 26th: Linderhof
June 27th to July 6th:
    June 27th to the 29th: Brunnenkopf
    June 30th to July 2nd?: Pürschling
    July 3rd to the 6th: Halbammer
July 7th to the 10th: Berg
July 11th to the 19th:
    July 11th to the 13th: Herzogstand?
    July 14th? to the 16th?: Sojern
    July 17th to the 19th: Grammersberg?
July 19th to August 21st:
    July 19th to the 20th: Berg
    July 21st to the 23rd: Kenzen
    July 23rd to August 18th: Hohenschwangau
    August 18th to the 21st: Tegelberg
August 21st to September 1st:
    August 21st to the 23rd: Linderhof
    August 24th to September 1st: Schachen
September 2nd to the 7th: Berg
September 8th to the 20th: Linderhof
September 20th to the 28th: Schachen
September 29th to October 8th:
    September 29th: Berg
    September 30th to October 8th: Herren-
    chiemsee
October 9th to the 14th: Berg
October 15th to the 30th:
    October 15th to the 26th: Linderhof
    October 27th to the 30th: Vorderriß
October 31st to November 13th: Munich
November 13th to December 31st:
    November 13th to the 15th: Linderhof
    November 16th to December 12th: Hohen-
    schwangau
    December 13th to the 21st: Linderhof
    December 22nd to the 31st: Hohen-
    schwangau

1884

January 1st to February 11th:
    January 1st to the 5th: Linderhof
    January 6th to the 22nd: Hohenschwangau
    January 23rd to the 31st: Linderhof
    February 1st to the 11th: Hohenschwangau
February 11th to May 11th:
    February 11th to the 12th: Partenkirchen
    February 12th to April 10th: Munich
    April 10th to the 24th: Hohenschwangau
    April 25th to May 11th: Munich
May 11th to the 14th: Berg
May 14th to the 18th?: Vorderriß – Hochkopf
May 19th to the 23rd: Linderhof
May 23rd to June 23rd:
    May 23rd to the 26th: Hohenschwangau
    May 27th to June 8th: Neuschwanstein (first longer sojourn!)
    June 9th to the 23rd: Hohenschwangau
June 24th to July 3rd:
    June 24th to the 27th: Brunnenkopf
    June 28th to the 30th: Pürschling
    July 1st: Berg
    July 1st to the 3rd: Halbammer?
July 4th to the 11th?: Linderhof
July 12th? to the 20th:
    July 12th? to the 14th: Herzogstand
    July 15th? to the 17th?: Sojern?
    July 18th? to the 20th: Grammersberg
July 21st to August 20th:
    July 21st to the 22nd: Berg
    July 23rd to the 25th: Kenzen
    July 26th to August 16th: Hohenschwangau and Neuschwanstein
    August 17th to the 20th: Tegelberg
August 21st to September 1st:
    August 20th to the 22nd: Linderhof
    August 23rd: Herrenchiemsee
    August 24th to September 1st: Schachen
September 2nd to the 7th: Berg
September 8th to the 20th?: Linderhof
September 21st to the 28th: Schachen
September 29th to October 9th:
    September 29th: Berg
    September 30th to October 9th: Herrenchiemsee
October 10th to the 15th: Berg

October 16th to the 30th:
    October 16th to the 26th?: Linderhof
    October 27th? to the 30th: Vorderriß
October 31st to November 13th: Munich
November 13th to December 31st:
    November 13th to the 15th: Linderhof
    November 16th to December 11th: Hohenschwangau/Neuschwanstein
    December 12th to the 21st: Linderhof
    December 22nd to the 31st: Hohenschwangau/Neuschwanstein

1885

January 1st to February 11th:
    January 1st to the 5th: Linderhof
    January 6th to the 9th: Hohenschwangau
    January 10th to the 23rd: Neuschwanstein
    January 23rd to the 31st: Linderhof
    February 1st to the 7th: Neuschwanstein
    February 7th to rhe 11th: Hohenschwangau
February 11th to May 11th:
    February 11th to the 12th: Partenkirchen
    February 12th to April 11th: Munich
    April 11th to the 25th: Hohenschwangau
    April 26th to May 11th: Munich
May 11th to the 14th: Berg
May 14th to the 18th: Vorderriß – Hochkopf
May 19th to the 23rd: Linderhof
May 24th to June 24th:
    May 24th to June 21st: Neuschwanstein
    June 22nd to the 24th: Hohenschwangau
June 25th to July 3rd?:
    June 25th to the 27th: Brunnenkopf
    June 28th to the 30th: Pürschling
    July 1st to the 3rd?:Halbammer
July 4th? to the 11th?: Linderhof
July 12th? to the 20th:
    July 12th? to the 14th?: Herzogstand?
    July 15th? to the 17th?: Sojern
    July 18th? to the 20th: Grammersberg?
July 21st to August 20th:
    July 21st to the 22nd: Berg
    July 23rd to the 25th: Kenzen
    July 26th to the 28th: Hohenschwangau
    July 29th to the August 14th: Neuschwanstein
    August 15th to the 17th: Hohenschwangau
    August 17th to the 20th: Tegelberg

August 20th to September 1st:
    August 20th to the 23rd: Linderhof
    August 24th to September 1st: Schachen
September 2nd to the 7th: Berg
September 8th to the 18th?: Linderhof
September 19th to the 27th: Schachen
September 28th to October 10th?:
    September 28th: Berg
    September 29th to October 10th?: Herren-
    chiemsee
October 11th to the 14th: Berg
October 14th to the 31st:
    October 14th to the 16th: Hohenschwangau
    October 16th to the 26th?: Linderhof
    October 27th? to the 31st: Vorderriß
October 31st to November 9th: Linderhof
November 10th to December 31st:
    November 10th to the 18th: Hohen-
    schwangau
    November 19th to December 13th:
    Neuschwanstein
    December 13th to the 21st: Linderhof
    December 22nd to the 31st: Hohenschwan-
    gau/Neuschwanstein

1886

January 1st to the 5th: Linderhof
January 6th to the 22nd: Hohenschwangau and
    Neuschwanstein
January 23rd to the 31st: Linderhof
February 1st to March 7th: Hohenschwangau and
    Neuschwanstein
March 8th to April 17th: Hohenschwangau
April 18th to May 8th: Neuschwanstein
May 9th to the 10th: Hohenschwangau
May 11th to the 14th: Berg
May 14th to the 18th: Vorderriß – Hochkopf[656]
May 19th to June 2nd: Linderhof
June 2nd to the 11th: Neuschwanstein.
On Sunday morning June 6th Ludwig II attend-
    ed mass at 6:00 a.m. in the chapel of the
    castle.
June 12th: At 4:30 in the morning a carriage of
    the state commissioner left Hohenschwan-
    gau with Ludwig II. It arrived in Schloss
    Berg at 12:12 p.m.
June 13th: Ludwig II dies in the Lake Starnberg.

Notes

1 Franz Merta, Ludwig II. und der Mobilmachungsbefehl von 1870 – Eine Richtigstellung irritierender Augenzeugenberichte, in: Zeitschrift für bayer. Landesgeschichte, vol. 48/3, 1985.
2 Compare Rall (Note 14) p 173.
3 Kurt Wilhelm, ed., Louise v. Kobell u. die Könige von Bayern. Munich 1980, p 263.
4 Karin and Hannes Heindl, Ludwigs heimliche Residenzen. Munich 1974, p 65.
5 Letter from Ludwig II to Richard Wagner, July 12th, 1876, see König Ludwig II und Richard Wagner. Briefwechsel. Edited by Otto Strobel. Karlsruhe 1936, vol. III, p 80.
6 Georg Hirth, Ludwig der Einsame, in: Die Jugend. Jg. 7,2. 1902, p 613.
7 Letter from Ludwig II to Richard Wagner, January 1st, 1872; compare (Note 5), vol. II, p 335.
8 Letter from Ludwig II to Richard Wagner, January 11th, 1876, ibid vol. III, p 72.
9 Letter from Ludwig II to Richard Wagner, July 12th, 1876, ibid vol. III, p 81.
10 Bayerischer Kurier 1872, p 2395.
11 Letter from Ludwig II to Richard Wagner, January 1, 1867; compare (Note 5), vol. II, p 205.
12 Letter from Ludwig II to Richard Wagner, August 21st, 1865, ibid vol. I, p 161.
13 Letter from Ludwig II to Cosima Wagner, July 21st, 1866; compare (Note 5), vol. II, p 75.
14 Letter from Ludwig II to Richard Wagner, November 24th, 1865; compare (Note 5), vol. I, p 221.
15 Letter from Ludwig II to Richard Wagner, August 4th, 1865, ibid vol. I p 142.
16 Letter from Ludwig II to Baroness von Leonrod, September 2nd, 1871, Geh. Hausarchiv Munich, Kabinettsakten Ludwigs II., 2.
17 See (Note 16), letter, March 31st, 1867.
18 Compare Rall (Note 16), Curtius vol. I, p 154.

19 See (Note 16), letter, December 30th, 1867.
20 Letter from Ludwig II to Prince Luitpold, October 31st and December 12th, 1870, Geh. Hausarchiv Munich, Private Papers of Prince Regent Luitpold 94.
21 See (Note 20), letter, December 9th, 1870.
22 See (Note 16), letter, July 16th, 1874.
23 See (Note 16), letter, March 24th, 1871.
24 Letter from Ludwig II to Cosima von Bülow, May 3rd, 1867, Geh. Hausarchiv, Munich, Kabinettsakten Ludwigs II., 139.
25 See (Note 20), letter, October 31st, 1870.
26 Walter Rummel, Ludwig II., 2nd printing 1930, p 48, Punkt III.
27 See (Note 20), letter, October 1st, 1870.
28 Peter Herde, Der Wechsel in der Münchner Nuntiatur 1874/75 und die bayerische Politik, in: Land und Reich, Stamm und Volk. Festgabe für Max Spindler zum 90. Geburtstag, vol. 3, Munich 1984, p 296 ff.
29 Letter from Ludwig II to Richard Wagner, May 26th, 1871; compare (Note 5), vol. III, p 324.
30 Letter from Ludwig II to Richard Wagner, August 30th, 1865, ibid vol. I, p 168 and p 120.
31 Felix Dahn, Errinnerungen, vol. 4, Leipzig 1895, p 316.
32 See (Note 31), p 313.
33 See (Note 16), letter, August 28th, 1870.
34 Paul v. Haufingen, Ludwig II., 2nd printing 1886, p 127 ff.
35 Letter from Ludwig II to Richard Wagner, June 5th, 1870; compare (Note 5), vol. II, p 309.
36 Letter from Ludwig II to Richard Wagner, January 1st, 1870, ibid vol. II, p 297.
37 Letter from Ludwig II to Richard Wagner, October 22nd, 1869, ibid vol. II, p 287 f.
38 G. v. Böhn, Ludwig II., 2nd printing Berlin 1924, p 445.
39 Letter from Ludwig II to Cosima v. Bülow, September 19th, 1866, Geh. Hausarchiv Munich, Kabinettsakten Ludwigs II., 138.
40 Letter from Ludwig II to Richard Wagner, June 5th, 1867; compare (Note 5), vol. II, p 173.
41 Letter from Ludwig II to Richard Wagner, August 30th, 1878, ibid vol. III, p 135.
42 Letter from Ludwig II to Richard Wagner, November 26th, 1882, ibid vol. III, p 255.
43 Letter from Ludwig II to Cosima v. Bülow, in March 1869, ibid vol. IV, p 196.
44 Letter from Ludwig II to Richard Wagner, September 18th, 1876, ibid vol. III, p 93.
45 Bayerisches Hauptstaatsarchiv Munich: Staatstheaterakt 856; see also Illus.
46 Compare (Note 5), vol. II, p 206.
47 Prinz Adalbert v. Bayern, Vier Revolutionen u. einiges dazwischen. Munich 1932, p 144.
48 Prof. Rall disassociates himself from some of the following sentences.
49 Letter from Ludwig II to Richard Wagner, August 9th, 1878; compare (Note 5), vol. III, p 132.
50 Letter from Ludwig II to Prince Luitpold, November 9th, 1871, Geh. Hausarchiv Munich: private papers Prince Regent Luitpold 94.
51 Compare (Note 5), vol. II, p 266.
52 Letter from Ludwig II to Richard Wagner, July 18th, 1866; compare (Note 5), vol. II, p 73.
53 Letter from Ludwig II to Richard Wagner, May 21st, 1867, ibid vol. II, p 171.
54 The papers dated "Schloss Berg, June 28th, 1865" were probably signed by the King at Linderhof. Supporting this argument are the two letters which Ludwig II wrote to Richard Wagner, the first dated June 27th, 1865 "Auf Bergshöhe (on the mountain)" and a second dated June 29th 1965 "Linderhof". – Compare (Note 5), vol. I, No. 98 and 100.
55 The papers dated "Schloss Berg, August 8th, 1866" were obviously taken along on a horseback trip and signed by the King while travelling. In a letter to Sophie dated August 9th, 1866 (Geh. Hausarchiv Munich, Kabinettsakten Ludwigs II., 88) Ludwig himself mentions just returning from a mountain excursion.
56 Though Edir Grein (Tagebuchaufzeichnungen Ludwigs II., Schaan 1925, p 119) places Ludwig for these days at Hohenschwangau he was probably, as usual, at Hochkopf, an argument supported by a comment in a letter to the Queen-mother Marie that it was recently gorgeous once again at Hochkopf (Chapman-Huston, Desmond: Bavarian fantasy. London 1955, p 276). Furthermore, the castle chronicle of Hohenschwangau which was carefully kept, does not register any comings or goings of Ludwig II's for these days at either Hohenschwangau or Neuschwanstein.